Stepping into the Light

Victory in Today's Culture

Stepping into the Light

© 1997 by David Wood

David Wood's Address is:
David Wood Ministries
P.O. Box 387
Trenton, GA 30752
or call 706/657-6043

ISBN 0-9660906-0-8

Cover and Book Design: Lee Fredrickson
Edited by Deborah K. Wood

Printed in the United States of America

Stepping into the Light

Victory in Today's Culture

David Wood

P.O. Box 8087 • Springfield, MO 65801

To my wife, June
An encourager
and to
"The Clan"
No man could have
a better
family.

Table of Contents

Introduction

When an electrical storm recently put out the lights in my home, I didn't curse the darkness. I reached for a flashlight.

As the forces of spiritual darkness sweep across America like shadows from a setting sun, too many believers have chosen to curse the darkness instead of reaching for a spiritual "flashlight." We have fallen for the ways of the world, frequently using the tools of the world in our attempts to organize, incorporate, and mobilize forces to fight the forces of darkness. And, too often, we fight this battle on the other side's turf.

Evangelist David Wood proposes another way.

Rather than focusing on the darkness, Wood points to a power source that is used more in name than in practice and calls us to step into that light—the light of Jesus Christ and the power of His Word.

A few years ago, a *USA Today* poll found that only 11 percent of the public reads the Bible daily. Larger percentages read it occasionally and twenty-two percent don't read it at all.

More recently, a George Barna Research survey found an appalling level of Biblical illiteracy, even among those who claim to believe the Bible is the Word of God. Barna reported that nearly two out of three adults agreed that "Satan is not a living being, but a symbol of evil." Most surprising, a majority of people who say they have been born again, deny Satan's existence.

It is the same with the Holy Spirit. Six in ten Americans surveyed agreed that, "the Holy Spirit is a symbol of God's presence or power, but is not a living entity." Again, an appallingly high number of people who identify themselves as born again agree with this statement. If people who are supposed to be children of the light walk in darkness, how can they expect to see clearly and lead others in the direction of the light?

If believers stopped trying to reform a dark world and began allowing themselves to be transformed by the light of

Christ, this light would shine so brightly in them and out from them that they would begin to lead many out of darkness. But as long as we focus on battling the world's problems with the world's ways, we will not succeed any better than our unbelieving friends who walk in darkness. Ask yourself who you would rather follow: someone still searching for matches to light a candle, or someone who has found a flashlight and can keep you from falling down the stairs.

We will not make this a better world. But we can make it a brighter world by allowing the light of Christ to shine out in practice, not just in our words. "See how they love one another," is a more powerful witness and far more effective than, "who do you like in the next presidential race?"

There are three beams of light that Jesus wants to shine through us. One is, "Love your enemies." This is a most unnatural form of behavior which immediately attracts attention from unbelievers, who live by the creed, "Don't get mad, get even."

"Pray for those who persecute you," opens a channel in your own heart through which God can operate. It is a kind of spiritual angioplasty, sparing us from anger and bitterness.

"Feed the hungry, clothe the naked and visit those in prison," not as ends in themselves, but as irresistible demonstrations of God's love that sheds an irresistible light into a person's dark corners.

These are the least tried of all Biblical principles. It is the reason the contemporary church has had a power failure and seeks to transform society through civil structures, rather than reform itself through obedience to its Lord. We have it backwards. We look for revival, but what we need is reformation, which then can bring revival.

David Wood's message is personal and it is active. It has behind it the authority of history. Each time believers have stepped into the light of Christ, the work of Jesus is advanced. Try stepping into the light yourself and watch how quickly the darkness dissipates.

—Cal Thomas
Syndicated Columnist, Washington, D.C.

9

Preface

I have a choice for you. I would like you to choose which of the following two men you'd rather be:

• James is the leading authority on cancer in this country. He knows all there is to know about it. The American Medical Association calls him with questions about cancer and James answers every one. James has been diagnosed with cancer.

• Phil, on the other hand, knows absolutely nothing about cancer; you could say he is completely ignorant on the subject. Yet, Phil does not have cancer.

Which of these men would you be, given the choice?

Why Phil, of course.

Up until three decades ago, Christians were a lot more like "Phils." They lived in the light, they loved the light, they lived by the light, and this kept the darkness at bay. Now we run around trying so hard to analyze and understand the horrible darkness of our world, that we are unknowingly allowing ourselves to become part of it, and it is defeating us. There are multitudes of Christians who can give appalling statistics about the horrible things happening in our country, but they cannot quote a Bible verse!

It is time, long past time, for a whole new outlook. Victory seems illusive at times, but it is vitally important to remember that "darkness" is the rule of our culture. The path into the light is not complicated. It is simple. It involves five basic steps, beginning with a realistic readjustment of our outlook on life, and ending with a step into positive service!

I invite you to sit down and "chat" with me, as I take a personal approach to this plan for victory. This book is intended as a nine-day study. Therefore a commitment is requested at the end of each chapter. It is suggested that you not read this whole book at one sitting, but read only a chapter or two at a time. Prepare your heart and mind to reflect upon, and digest this plan, which is practical and exciting. Get ready for a blessing!

Stepping Into The Light is an exciting and powerful adjustment, both spiritually and mentally, for a Christian to make! The end result? Success!!

—David A. Wood

John 8:12

"Then spake Jesus again unto them, saying, I am the light of the world: he that followeth me shall not walk in darkness, but shall have the light of life."

Chapter One

A Whole New Outlook

Two men looked out of prison bars;
one saw mud, the other saw stars.

So, you are worried about the moral climate in America. I am worried, too. You simply cannot believe how far the liberals and the Hollywood entertainers have gone. You say you are concerned that our children do not have good role models as leaders. You are scared to death of what they are learning in school. You are not alone.

To make matters worse, you are just not living a life of personal victory. Every time you make a firm resolve, it seems to breaks down somewhere in the middle of the morning newspaper.

As you know, these are modern times. In the world of literature, it is called postmodernism; in art, it is abstractionism or surrealism; in music, who knows?! We are living in a time that is absolutely exploding with brand new horrendous problems, both moral and political. The problems run rampant in our government, in our cities, and in our homes. It is a time fraught with peer pressure, intense adolescent sexuality, high abortion and divorce rates, and nearly every kind of "social" disease possible.

We are also living in a time when it is vital for Christians to do a complete "about face" and claim victory over the darkness that surrounds them. In other words, it is time for a whole new outlook!

One of the most tremendous truths taught in the Word of God is the wonderful principle that God did not save us to be victims; He saved us to be victors! I wish I could miraculously ingrain that upon your heart and your mind right now, so that you could immediately live the victorious life God has for you.

In this first chapter, we are going to lay the foundation for the rest of the book. Later on, we will be learning how to conquer obstacles, and how to dispel discouragement and insecurity. But first, we must understand our gifts from God and our responsibility to Him.

Our journey begins in I Corinthians 13:13, which reads, "And now abideth faith, hope, charity, these three; but the greatest of these is charity." Note very carefully the word "charity." This, of course, is our word "love," agape in the beautiful Greek.

God is making both a statement and a promise in this verse. Notice the verb tense that is used: "now abideth." Literally, that is what is called the present durative active tense. This means that the action described has a point of beginning, but it never ends. It is something that wonderfully starts in your life, and it continues to go and it continues to grow! That is exactly what God is telling us about faith, hope, and love.

In fact, we can read of another great promise in Philippians 1:6, when God says, "Being confident of this very thing, that he which hath begun a good work in you will perform it until the day of Jesus Christ:"

This is just as relevant today as when it was first written in the First Century. I am sure that every dedicated Christian will admit that the upcoming move into the 21st century must be made with victory and confidence. But how? How do we fully trust that we can win the lost? How can we be effective for God in our communities and in our country? How can we have the solid homes that we desire? How can our relationships with our spouses be holy, sanctified, happy unions? There are just too many other distracting things going on, right?

Think with me for a moment about areas in which you need personal victory. Most likely, you are thinking of times when you made a commitment. You started working towards it, and then for some reason you just stopped. A short while later, the Holy Spirit convicted you. So you started again... then you stopped. Is that what's coming to mind right now? I would like you to stop reading for a moment and think—be specific, and be practical.

You know, God does not have our human quality of starting something and stopping in the middle. As we saw in the Scripture earlier, He "will perform" and can perform what He promises the Believer until the day of His coming. Amen! But while we are here on earth, we have a constant struggle with Self. Were you able to think of any areas in your life wherein you struggle for the victory?

How about reading the Bible every day? Did you know the devil defeats you by telling you that you are the only Christian who has a problem in this area? Every Christian has a hard time doing this; it takes real discipline. How many times have you committed to reading the Bible through in a year? How many times have you stopped in March or April because you have fallen so far behind?

Has Satan come up behind you at these times and "rung your bell?" "Look at you," he whispers, "some kind of Christian you are, you can't even get up fifteen minutes earlier to read your Bible... No one else has that problem." Have you noticed that if you listen to him, the joy and victory will begin to dwindle away from other areas in your life as well? That is his evil plan!

It is not just you who has a problem being consistent. That is the case with every born again child of God! Satan does not want you to be consistent in your Christian life.

What about your prayer life? I believe that prayer is probably the one single greatest source of power that God's people never use. It saddens me to think that Christians will get to Heaven one day, and there we will find that we wasted this wonderful asset. We just did not use it faithfully. You have heard the medical studies that prove we only use a tiny percentage of our brains, and about how powerful we would be if we could somehow "tap" into the rest of our mental potential. That is the way I picture prayer!

Prayer affects every aspect of our relationship with God: we fellowship with Him, we worship Him, we seek answers on our faces before Him, we thank Him for answers to our problems.... yet we are usually so needy in this area! How often have you had to go before the Lord and say, "Lord, forgive me; I've been ignoring You?"

Here is another very important area: soul winning. How many times have you mentally kicked yourself because you are not going out and sharing your faith with others the way you should? Is witnessing hard for you?

A preacher friend of mine was in a restaurant in Oklahoma one Sunday after a crusade service. The table conversation centered on soul winning. One of the gentlemen present remarked that, to him, the prospect of going out soul winning was the same as knowing he was going to the gym to work out; all of a sudden, anything in the world becomes more important, and you just never go.

In this area, as well, it takes real discipline. Even Christians who are successful soul winners, who are personally acquainted with the wonderful joy they experience when they lead others to Christ, have to fight a battle with Self, and win, before they go out witnessing. I know. I have been there. You have been there too, haven't you? You get started, then you stop. The Holy Spirit convicts. You get started again; then you stop again. Finally, you may just give up. What a tragedy!

What is another area where help is needed today? It is the basic social unit of all society, including our local churches, and it is crumbling all around us. I am sure you have thought of it by now: it's the Christian home. Sadly, one of our most neglected institutions is the family. We need victory in our family lives, in our husband/wife relationships, and in our parent/child relationships.

You may be saying right now, "Hold it! Are you telling me that you're going to give me, in this one book, everything I need to have victory in every area of my life?" That is absolutely true!

You see, it is not complicated. One of our problems

today is that we tend to over-complicate issues that are basically simple. We say to ourselves, "O.K., I need victory in Bible reading and prayer; that means I must master 57 different things." Or, "I need to have victory in my family life. I'll make a long list, and I'll work at it. Then, if I ever get through the list, maybe one day I'll have the victory for which I long."

We go to our meetings, and we ask what we need to know to be a good soul winner. "Well," somebody answers, "There are volumes written on that subject; there are at least 150 things you need to know..." Has that ever happened to you?

You get so frustrated, and so depressed, thinking that this is all too much and you just cannot do it. You think it is impossible, because you are already juggling your job and wrestling with your finances. Maybe it is only the pastor who experiences true victory, you think, and he went to college to learn how. So, you just do not even try to live the truly victorious spiritual life.

Do you know why?

Because inspiration without education always leads to frustration.

Yet there are few courses in college, or anywhere in academia, that teach you how to live a victorious life. That is not God's approach at all. He has not complicated victory —He has not designed it like some sort of college degree, so that one day you will make the grade and "graduate" into victory. He makes it simple because He wants you to experience it!

When I received the Lord as my Savior at age nineteen, one of the first desires I had was to have victory in my Christian life. To me, at that time, "victory" meant victory over temptation, victory over sin, and strength to accomplish the things in my life that I knew God wanted done.

These were not regimented, legalistic steps in life as much as they were areas that I personally knew needed to be corrected in order for me to do what I wanted to do, as well as what He wished for me.

At that time, I became acquainted with such spiritual authors as Watchman Nee, Andrew Murray, and Dr. L.E. Maxwell. In fact, I read Dr. Maxwell's book on being crucified, which focused on Galatians 2:20, twice. I also became acquainted with Keswick teachers and preachers, who had ministered at great Christian conferences focusing on areas we sometimes refer to as "the deeper life."

My general impression, at that time, was that spirituality was a maturity plane that could be reached by a deep grasp of the Scripture, as well as a lifestyle that was a little beyond my comprehension.

I thank the Lord for what He taught me and what I was able to apply from this period, but struggled with getting a "handle" on the "how-to." Through these years, God led me to look at some very practical teachings in the Word of God. The result of that careful study is the basis for all of the teaching, training, and approaches you will find in this simple book.

I began to see that if I would exercise a daily, deliberate, conscious decision to follow a practical plan found in God's Word, the victory I had so desired would become a reality. Over time, and many incidents, experiences and lessons I learned in life, this plan fell beautifully into place.

I have now found, as all Christians have, that no one is perfect and we never can do everything right all the time. However, I have also found a general and genuine excitement, and encouragement, and an extremely positive approach to life through applying the Biblical principles in this plan for victory in the Christian life. That is why I had to share it with you!

You are going to learn one approach in this book, and only one.

Consider our verse in I Corinthians again. This section of Scripture, from chapter 12 to chapter 14, deals with spiritual gifts, and how the Holy Spirit gives us power to accomplish our greatest for God. Sandwiched right in the middle is chapter 13, or the "love chapter." Here God gives us practical approaches on how love is to be exemplified in our lives. Verse 13 of this chapter is the pivotal verse of the entire section. It is the one verse on which all of the rest are built.

God says that now, right now, at the turn of the new century, in the midst of all the confusion and depression that surrounds us, "now abideth faith, hope, and charity...." What do you know! There is something that is abiding, something to count on!

Remember, there is a point at which it starts in your life, when you accept Christ as your Savior, but there is no point at which it stops.

I ask you to consider something else about this verse: it is not really in the Scripture for what I like to call "deep theological reasons," although every verse in the Bible teaches great truth. It is also not in the Bible for philosophical reasons, in order to give someone a different approach to life than somebody else. Guess what? It's not there for poetic reasons either, even though there is an old Sunday School song written about it. Do you remember it? (This will date you!)

> *Faith, hope, and charity,*
> *That's the way to live successfully.*
> *How do I know?*
> *The Bible tells me so.*

Verse 13 is there to be what I call "spiritual preventive maintenance." What is preventive maintenance? I ask this question all the time when I am conducting crusades. The best definition I have heard was from a dear lady in North Carolina, who stood and said, "Preventive maintenance is when you fix something that is small before it becomes something that is big." Isn't that great? It'd be difficult to say it any better!

God is teaching us that there are things we can do in our lives, little things, that will keep us from having major breakdowns!

We have all seen the old commercial that used to be aired a great deal during sporting events: the greasy mechanic rolls out from under the automobile on a creeper, looks directly at the camera, and solemnly says, "Pay me now, or pay me later!"

You know from your own experience that you have to service your car, you have to change the oil, you have to balance and rotate the tires once in awhile. You have to spend a few dollars and a little bit of time **now**, or you will have a major breakdown **later**.

What about it?

In your opinion, are we Christians having major breakdowns today? You know as well as I do that we are, and it is affecting our impact on this world. We are having these breakdowns because we are not giving attention to **spiritual preventive maintenance**.

You see, verse 13 is not saying that this faith, hope, and love abideth for our pleasure, that it's a "free ride," that we have no responsibility. We do. We have to renew them daily.

Did you hear about the businessman who got sick and tired of taking a shower and getting dressed every single morning? Well, here is what he did a couple of months ago: he took a very long, hot shower, and used the most expensive shampoo and soap he could find. When he got dressed, he took special care and didn't wrinkle anything. He then worked on his hair until it was absolutely perfect, and brushed his teeth until they shone.

When he felt he could not improve a thing, he stood back and looked at himself in the mirror. "There," he said smugly to himself, "Now you have done it so well that you'll never have to do it again!" And he hasn't! (I'm sure you believe that!)

That is a little silly, but it clearly illustrates the point I am making about spiritual preventive maintenance. It is just like the lady who has to put her makeup on every single morning; you do not do it just once.

I am reminded of a story my daughter told me some years ago. She was home for Christmas break from college in Virginia, and was confused about an incident that had occurred with her roommate.

Her roommate (we'll call her Brenda) received a phone call from home one evening and was literally sobbing when she got off the phone. My daughter asked what was wrong and was told that the girl's dog, Rusty, had just died.

"He was so cute and friendly, and we all loved him so much!" Brenda sobbed.

"What happened to him?" My daughter asked.

"The doctor said he contracted some kind of canine virus, and it turned into pneumonia, and they couldn't save him."

"That's terrible," my daughter said, as she tried to comfort her friend, "I thought all those shots they get when they are puppies keep them from getting sick like that."

"Oh," Brenda responded, "We never took him to the doctor for shots and checkups and stuff. My dad always says that's a waste of time and money."

No wonder my daughter was confused! This is another example of the preventive maintenance we must have in our lives. And it is even more important in our spiritual lives.

We will be dealing with this spiritual preventive maintenance over the next eight chapters. I am going to be asking you to turn on three different "light switches" in your mind and heart, because everyone knows the only force that drives out darkness is light. Make a promise to God, and to yourself, before starting chapter two, that you will step into the light. I trust you are as excited as I am!

FAITH
Matthew 17:20

"And Jesus said unto them, Because of your unbelief: for verily I say unto you, If ye have faith as a grain of mustard seed, ye shall say unto this mountain, Remove hence to yonder place; and it shall remove; and nothing shall be impossible unto you."

Chapter Two

Stepping Into Faith

*You should never abandon your faith when it
weakens, anymore than you would throw away
a suit that needs to be drycleaned.*

*Never doubt in the dark
what God told you in the light.*

Did you know that you do not have to have great faith?
I hear so many people say, "Oh, if I had the faith of
D.L. Moody...," or, "If I had the faith of John R. Rice, who
founded The Sword of the Lord...," or, "If only I could be
like George Mueller, who prayed millions in money and
supplies to support a wonderful orphanage... ." They mention Evangelist Billy Sunday, courageous Corrie Ten Boom,
martyr Jim Elliot, missionary William Carey, and others.
They speak of all the things they could do for God if they
only had the faith of these spiritual giants.

But Jesus tells us in Matthew 17:20, that if we have
faith that is the size of a grain of mustard seed (you can
barely see a grain of mustard seed, by the way), that we can
move mountains.

In Deuteronomy 32:20, the Lord says, ... "I will hide
my face from them, I will see what their end shall be: for
they are a very froward generation, children in whom is no
faith." Does that ring any bells for you? Maybe it reminds
you a little of what's going on in our country today.

Perhaps you have noticed the way a little child trusts
a parent; maybe it is true in your own parenting experience. You can hold that child's hand and lead him into any
situation, no matter how dark or scary, and the child

completely trusts you! What are the two powerful words you say, words that completely calm the little one's fears? "Everything's okay." God wants us to trust Him just like this! What is wrong with our faith, then? What is the secret?

The key is that you have to make sure, every single day, that your faith is renewed. Every morning you must get up and say, "God, I'm going to trust you today, all day. I'm going to let you be the reigning, supreme influence in my life and my decisions today." Here it is again: **spiritual preventive maintenance**.

Let's look at what the Bible says about faith:

"Now faith is the substance of things hoped for, the evidence of things not seen" (Hebrews 11:1).

"But without faith it is impossible to please him:..." (Hebrews 11:6).

"But let him ask in faith, nothing wavering. For he that wavereth is like a wave of the sea driven with the wind and tossed" (James 1:6).

"Knowing this, that the trying of your faith worketh patience" (James 1:3).

"I have fought a good fight, I have finished my course, I have kept the faith" (2 Timothy 4:7).

"I have kept the faith." That's one of my favorite declarations of victory in the Bible! Paul knew that it was his responsibility to renew his faith daily by simply promising God that he would trust Him, no matter what.

I have given you five verses that deal with faith. Did you know that the Scofield Reference Edition of the King James Version of the Bible lists 136 references to faith in its concordance, and that the word really appears over 250 times in the New Testament alone? Do you think faith is important to God? Yes, it is most important!

The first "light switch" I am going to ask you to turn on is the light switch of faith. Picture a dark room in your mind right now and ask yourself the following question: What is the only way to drive out this darkness?

I want to illustrate this with a hypothetical situation. Normally, when I am going to be conducting a crusade in a church with which I am unfamiliar, I like to go to the church building on Saturday evening and look around the auditorium. It gives me a certain "feel" for the place to see it empty, and to kneel in prayer at the altar asking for God's blessings on the crusade.

Suppose one Saturday a pastor picks me up at the airport and drives me to the church, and during the entire drive he simply raves about the great new auditorium the Lord has allowed him and his people to build. When we arrive, he eagerly leads me in the front doors, through the foyer, and into the back of this brand new, gorgeous auditorium.

Well, it is pitch black inside! I stand there for a few moments with the pastor beside me. Finally I say, "Pastor, I can't see a thing." He responds immediately with, "That's right, it is dark in here!" He begins walking down the aisle away from me, flailing his hands at the darkness, trying to push it away and yelling, "Get out of here, darkness! We can't see!"

If you were standing there at the back of the dark auditorium, listening to him yelling at the darkness, what would you say? You might suggest "Excuse me, Pastor, but if you want to get rid of the darkness, all you have to do is turn on the light."

There it is in a nutshell! That is the most important principle you will learn in this book! Remember, "darkness" in the Bible is error; "light" in the Bible is the truth of the Word of God. Very simply, it is up to us to walk in the light, to continually turn on the light switch of faith. It is the only way to be victorious in today's culture.

In John 3:19, Jesus says, "And this is the condemnation,

that light is come into the world, and men loved darkness rather than light, because their deeds were evil." Loving the light, walking in the light—it is a choice we must make! And we need to make it daily!

Did you know that darkness is terrified of light? You have no need to fear the darkness, because all you have to do is turn on the light and it holds the darkness out of your life.

That is the reason why our public school system will not let balanced creationism be taught in the classroom; they are scared to death of the light! They know that as soon as you let the light of truth in, darkness is driven out.

For instance, let us sit twenty students in a classroom who have never heard of the Bible and know nothing about creation. Let's have a creation scientist teach creationism, then we will have an evolution scientist teach evolutionism, and what do you think will happen? The students will turn to the light. They have taken it out of schools, because the devil must have darkness before he can work.

At the end of chapter one I told you I was going to ask you to turn on three light switches in your life and that together they will drive out darkness. Light switch #1 is faith. Here is an obvious question: if we are going to have victory, and we consciously "turn on" the light switch of faith, what area of darkness will we drive out?

Let us look at a wonderful story found in Luke 8:40-48. Take a moment and turn to that chapter in your Bible and highlight it. Here is a little trick I learned a long time ago: Later on today, or in the next couple of days, tell this story to someone in your own words—it's a great way to understand the Bible, and to be able to picture yourself right there in the story. Take a moment now to read these verses before continuing on in this chapter.

"And it came to pass, that, when Jesus was returned, the people gladly received him: for they were all waiting for him. And, behold, there came a man named Jairus, and he was a ruler of the synagogue: and he fell down at

Jesus' feet, and besought him that he would come into his house: For he had one only daughter, about twelve years of age, and she lay a dying. But as he went the people thronged him. And a woman having an issue of blood twelve years, which had spent all her living upon physicians, neither could be healed of any, Came behind him, and touched the border of his garment: and immediately her issue of blood stanched. And Jesus said, Who touched me? When all denied, Peter and they that were with him said, Master, the multitude throng thee and press thee, and sayest thou, Who touched me? And Jesus said, Somebody hath touched me: for I perceive that virtue is gone out of me. And when the woman saw that she was not hid, she came trembling, and falling down before him, she declared unto him before all the people for what cause she had touched him, and how she was healed immediately. And he said unto her, Daughter, be of good comfort: thy faith hath made thee whole; go in peace."

– Luke 8:40-48

This is a story from the life of a man named Jairus, who was a ruler in the synagogue. Jairus had a problem. His 12-year-old daughter was very sick; in fact, she "lay a dying."

I have four children, and I don't know how you would respond, but if I received word that one of my children was sick unto death, I would be desperate. Jairus knew exactly what to do; he went directly to Jesus. He told Jesus his problem and begged for His help.

While Jairus was trying to get Jesus to come to his house, in the middle of a huge crowd, a woman approached them from behind. This woman had an "issue of blood," or what we would call a blood disorder; she had spent all of her money trying to get help from doctors. She bent over and touched the hem of Jesus' garment as He was walking, and she was gloriously healed. Jesus then did something that I believe Jairus did not want him to do: He stopped.

Can you imagine how agitated Jairus must have been while Jesus was talking with His disciples and this woman? I do not know how long he had to wait, but while he was standing there, one of his servants came up to him and said, "Thy daughter is dead; trouble not the Master."

Can you imagine the grief that must have hit Jairus in that instant! Do you think he expected Jesus to turn to him and calmly say, "Fear not: believe only?" Certainly not.

When I was just starting out as a pastor, I was terrified because I wasn't from a Christian home. I had not had a lot of Christian friends and influence in my life. So I studied my Bible, and made a decision that no matter what happened, I would deal with every situation **exactly** as Jesus would have dealt with it. Then I would be safe. Well it was a good idea, and it worked fine, until I faced my first death in the church. What did Jesus do when He encountered death? Yes, He raised the person from the dead. Don't waste your time. I tried it; it doesn't work (there is only one "Great Physician")!

You see, in all instances of Jesus' public life, He not only loved unconditionally and consistently lived a perfect life example for us, but He also constantly taught life-changing lessons. What He said to Jairus in front of the pressing multitude was basically this: You can have faith and believe, OR you can have fear. But you cannot have fear and faith at the same time!

Do you see it? You cannot have fear and faith abiding inside of you at the same time, because one is darkness and the other is light!

Of course Jairus' faith was rewarded.

About fifteen years ago, when I was pastoring in Michigan, a couple in my church came to me for marriage counseling. Their problems were so extreme that I decided to counsel them separately at first. I will never forget my first session with the young lady.

Her husband had hurt her terribly, but he had admitted his mistakes and had begged her forgiveness. She sat in my office and said that she could not understand why their marriage was still in such a mess.

"Have you forgiven him?" I asked.

"Of course I have," she assured me. During the next few moments, however, I listened to her say four different things that she wished would happen to this man. She was dropping phrases such as, "That would teach him a lesson," and, "Then he'll know how it feels."

"You have not forgiven your husband," I said, "Because a spirit of forgiveness and a spirit of revenge cannot dwell in the same heart. It's impossible."

We went on to study the Bible together and she became broken over her own fault in their problems. The couple became wonderfully reconciled, and are still happy today.

Just as forgiveness and revenge cannot coexist in the human soul, so it is the same for faith and fear! It's impossible.

Let me tell you something else: you do not have to understand fear in order to have victory over it. Fear is the darkness that is driven out when you turn on the light switch of faith!

Will you commit to God before reading on any further in this book, that you will **make a choice**, from now on, to walk in faith? Look into your heart right now, and picture that light switch with the word F-A-I-T-H written on it. Reach out and flip that switch; promise yourself that you will not allow the darkness of fear to reside in you.

You must also remember to use your **spiritual preventive maintenance**—turn that light switch on every single day. Renew your faith, and promise God you'll trust Him.

Turning on the light switch of faith drives out fear, and fear is the main force that keeps you from overcoming the obstacles in your life.

Fear causes people to draw back from situations;
it brings on mediocrity; it dulls creativity;
it sets one up to be a loser in life.
- Fran Tarkenton

FAITH
Isaiah 41:10

"Fear thou not; for I am with thee: be not dismayed; for I am thy God: I will strengthen thee; yea, I will help thee; yea, I will uphold thee with the right hand of my righteousness."

Chapter Three

The Step Over Obstacles

*Obstacles are those frightening things you see
when you take your eyes off the goal.*

*A gauge of success is not whether you
have a tough problem,
But whether it's the same problem
that you had last year.*

I am going to give you another key right now. I am going
to tell you how you can live a life of absolute failure. Do
you want to know how every obstacle in your life can
become so insurmountable that you never have victory
over them? Basically, what I am going to share with you is
how you can join the ranks of those other people in society:
the victims.

You have heard them; everything is always someone
else's fault. "It is the government's fault," or, "It is because
of the way I was raised," or, "We cannot punish this crimi-
nal, he is just a product of his environment..." Guess what
the big secret is? They are living a life of FEAR. They have
developed a victim complex. Even the most dedicated
Christians must guard against feeling sorry for themselves.

I had a young man tell me after a service one evening
that he just could not stand the way people in the church
would talk about him when he tried to do something for
God. He had a neighborhood ministry going around per-
forming Gospel puppet shows and witnessing for Christ.
Many children were getting saved and coming to church,
yet he was receiving backlash from gossip and innuendos.
This, of course, hurt him.

I smiled and told him, "If I have learned anything in the forty-some-odd years I've been alive, it is simply this: there is only one way to never have anyone talk about you, or not to have suspicions about you—never do anything, never have anything, never know anything."

The Webster's II New College Dictionary defines an obstacle as something "that opposes, stands in the way of, or deters passage or progress." That sums it up for me, how about you?

Have you ever heard anyone refer to life as an obstacle course? The dictionary defines an obstacle course as a "situation full of obstacles that must be overcome." Did you catch that? ".....obstacles that must be overcome."

People also refer to obstacles as "burdens." So many have come up to me at crusades saying, "Brother Wood, please pray for me." I ask, "Why do you need prayer?" They usually sigh heavily and say something like, "Well, I'm under such a burden."

I always long to say, "What in the world are you doing down there?" Remember, God saved us to be victors, not victims!

Since we are dealing with obstacles in this chapter, I want to ask you a question: do you have to understand an obstacle before you can overcome it?

Let's take this to a more literal level with a simple illustration. You and a friend are out walking through a shady path in the woods. You are busy talking and enjoying the late afternoon sunshine as it slants through the trees. You turn a corner and right in front of you a tree trunk is lying across the path. So, the two of you sit down on the path in front of the tree.

"Maybe a storm blew it over," you say.

"I don't know," your friend rejoins, "If you look down here at the bottom, you can see ax marks. I think someone cut it down."

"Hmmmm, that's very interesting. What kind of a tree do you think it is?" you ask.

"Well, it has pine needles, so I believe it's a pine," your

friend answers. After spending time discussing the type of tree, and all the reasons you can imagine for it being there, the two of you decide that maybe you should get back to your walk.

"I guess we should get going," you say, "but maybe we should touch the tree before we step over it."

I know that is a ridiculous situation, and that in reality you would have rounded the corner and stepped over the tree without breaking stride. But look how the analogy fits in our lives!

You have heard the old saying, "The only thing we have to fear is fear itself." To a certain extent, that is true. Fear turns every difficulty into an obstacle and will rob your life of victory.

But you do not have to fear it, and you do not have to fight it. All you have to do is make sure that the light switch of faith stays "**on**."

Did you know that it is a sin not to have faith? The Bible says in Romans 14:23, that "whatsoever is not of faith is sin."

I gave you a choice in the preface to this book. I asked you if you would rather be James, who is the leading authority on cancer in this country, and has cancer; or Phil, who knows nothing about cancer, yet he does not have it. That is exactly what I am talking about when I say you do not have to understand your fear, or the obstacles in your path, in order to overcome them. What you do have to understand is that obstacles are common to everyone in the world, and that you cannot have victory in your life unless you overcome them.

I propose to you that one of society's biggest problems is that we are all trying too hard to understand the obstacles, and that has taken us off the path. Years ago, we did not need to understand all about the problem, but we sure did understand the solution!

Why have the tables turned so drastically? We have become a society that is being "seminared" and "psychic hotlined" to death. I do not have anything against seminars;

they should be used for training purposes. But it seems today that in most cases all we are doing is studying the problems. Never before have Christians had the opportunity to buy as many books, attend as many seminars, and study as many problems as they have today.

Have you noticed that Christians are calling sin by the same names which the world is using today? We know everything about the problems, but the sad part is, in our close analysis, we often contract them.

In fact, if I were going to be politically correct and fit into today's culture, I would not even be calling fear "fear." You know what I would be calling it? That popular word, "phobia."

People today have the appropriate number of phobias. People even seem to be proud of them! It is like the person who gets out of the hospital after having surgery and wants to show everyone his scars.

It's on the news, on the talk shows, on the "hard copy" shows: everyone is terrified of old age, or of being closed in, or of being in open spaces, or of being in a crowd, or of being alone, and the list goes on. We are giving our children "ritalin" because they are too hyper and their attention spans are not long enough. We are taking sleeping pills to get to sleep at night. If there is nothing to be afraid of, we will make something up.

Did you know that even the news and the weather forecasts are reported on what they call a "fear bias?" Today, they're calling it a 92% bias. This means that you can go outside and see that it is a gorgeous day; the sun is shining, the birds are chirping, and it is beautiful. Then what happens? You watch the weather report and feel like you ought to be hiding yourself, because the sky is falling.

I was watching the local news recently. They had a special way of starting the newscast called "Ten at Ten." That meant in the first ten minutes of the show, they told the top ten stories of the day. After watching those ten minutes, which was one negative report after another, I said, "Wow, these people are trying to scare me to death!"

Here's a phrase that's overused in our culture: "What if?" We "what if?" everything. "I would do this, but what if this happens?" "What if I lose my job one day?" "I want to marry her, but what if she stops loving me one day?" We've "what iffed" ourselves into a corner of fear. It's no wonder we are defeated in our lives!

Now, if you are not throwing this book down right now, you're probably asking me, "Aren't you a realist? Don't you watch the news? Aren't taxes eating you alive? Aren't interest rates killing you? Aren't you saddened by all of the violent killings reported on the news? What about AIDS? Aren't you scared of what is happening to our country?"

Of course I am a realist, but I am a realist who walks by faith! As Solomon said in Ecclesiastes 1:9, "...there is no new thing under the sun." There have always been problems. There always will be. Why don't you make sure that you are living clean before God and doing all you can for Him everyday, and then let God take care of the rest? Trust in Him!

"Trust in the Lord with all thine heart; and lean not unto thine own understanding.

In all thy ways acknowledge him, and he shall direct thy paths" (Proverbs 3:5,6).

Jesus is coming back, and He has everything under control. Do you believe that? In Genesis 18:14, God asked Abraham, "Is any thing too hard for the Lord?" You have to answer that question in your own life. If you believe this wholeheartedly, the fear cannot reign inside of you.

If obstacles constantly get you down, consider the following, which is taken from an excellent book, *Chicken Soup for the Soul:*

◆ After Fred Astaire's first screen test, a 1933 memo from the MGM testing director said: "Can't act. Slightly bald. Can dance a little." Astaire kept that memo over his fireplace in his Beverly Hills home.

◆ An expert said once of famous football coach Vince Lombardi: "He possesses minimal football knowledge. Lacks motivation."

◆ Louisa May Alcott, the author of *Little Women,* was advised by her family to find work as a servant or seamstress.

◆ Beethoven handled the violin awkwardly and preferred playing his own compositions instead of improving his technique. His teacher called him "hopeless as a composer."

◆ The teacher of famous opera singer Enrico Caruso said Caruso had no voice at all and could not sing.

◆ Walt Disney was fired by a newspaper for lacking ideas. He also went bankrupt several times before he built Disneyland.

◆ Eighteen publishers turned down Richard Bach's 10,000-word story about a soaring seagull before Macmillan finally published it in 1970. By 1975, *Jonathan Livingston Seagull* had sold more than seven million copies in the U.S. alone.

How's that for encouraging? Here is one of my favorites for reading when I need a personal lift (try to guess whose record it is as you are reading it):

Incident	**Age**
Failed in Business	22
Ran for Legislature - Defeated	23
Again Failed in Business	24
Elected to Legislature	25
Sweetheart Died	26
Suffered a Nervous Breakdown	27
Defeated for Speaker of the House	29
Defeated for Elector	31
Defeated for Congress	34
Elected to Congress	37
Defeated for Congress	39
Defeated for Senate	46
Defeated for Vice-President	47
Defeated for Senate	49
Elected President of the United States	51

It's the record of Abraham Lincoln!!

This business of conquering obstacles by refusing to live in fear is very serious, and it's very necessary.

Before we leave the subject of stepping into faith and stepping away from fear, I want you to realize and take to heart, the following principles from the Bible:

1) Faith always precedes understanding.

"Through faith we understand that the worlds were framed by the word of God, so that things which are seen were not made of things which do appear" (Hebrews 11:3).

2) Faith also always precedes accomplishment.

"And these all, having obtained a good report through faith, ..." (Hebrews 11:39).

3) Faith always precedes salvation.

"For by grace are ye saved through faith; and that not of yourselves: it is the gift of God: Not of works, lest any man should boast" (Ephesians 2:8, 9).

4) But, faith is always preceded by the Word of God.

"So then faith cometh by hearing, and hearing by the word of God" (Romans 10:17).

In other words, you must have faith in your inner life in order to have victory. But you cannot have faith, or increase your faith, if you do not read the Bible. That is why Bible reading is so important!

I am appalled by the number of Christians today who do not read the Bible. They can give you that list of statistics showing how horrible the situation in the world is today, but they cannot quote a Bible verse. (Well, maybe John 3:16, but little else of God's Word is filed away in the heart, ready for the Holy Spirit to bring to their remembrance.)

Will you take a moment right now to get alone with God? Look deep into the quiet chamber of your heart, turn on the light switch of faith, and simply say, "God, I believe you."

Make a commitment right now that you are going to be a person who walks by faith! Read this statement aloud, "Where there is faith there is no fear." Say it over and over to yourself today, and tomorrow, and the next day, until it is ingrained upon your heart and mind.

When Peter was in the midst of the storm, and was walking on the water, when was the only time he started to sink? **When he took his eyes off Jesus**.

We, too, are in the midst of the storm: storms of alcohol, drug abuse, violence, sexual immorality. These storms beset us on every side. We must keep looking up at the "author and finisher of our faith" (Hebrews 12:2). Step over those obstacles without looking down and keep marching on to victory!

HOPE
Romans 5:2-5

"By whom also we have access by faith into this grace wherein we stand, and rejoice in hope of the glory of God. And not only so, but we glory in tribulations also: knowing that tribulation worketh patience; And patience, experience; and experience, hope: And hope maketh not ashamed; because the love of God is shed abroad in our hearts by the Holy Ghost which is given unto us."

Chapter Four

Stepping Into Hope

The world hopes for the best,
but Jesus Christ offers the best hope.
- John Wesley White

Iam going to introduce you to the second light switch: hope.

Let us return to our foundational verse, 1 Corinthians 13:13. "And now abideth faith, hope, charity, these three; but the greatest of these is charity."

We have already flipped on the light switch of faith, and found that it drives out the darkness of fear. We have established that through spiritual preventive maintenance, we keep little things from piling up like debris in our lives; it is a constant renewal process.

Do you remember another Sunday School song? It is one of my favorites. I feel a thrill every time I pass the open door of a first or second grade Sunday School class and hear the children's sweet, clear voices singing it.

Every day with Jesus
Is sweeter than the day before.
Every day with Jesus
I love Him more and more.
Jesus saves and keeps me,
And He's the one I'm waiting for.
Every day with Jesus
Is sweeter than the day before.

Did you catch that line, "He's the one I'm waiting for?" That is the entire essence of hope.

Before reading any further, I want to ask you to do

something. Get a piece of paper and a pen, then write down your definition of hope. After you do this, come back and we will continue.

Did you get the key in your definition? Webster's defines hope as, "A wish or desire accompanied by confident expectation of its fulfillment." This is the key: confidently expecting the wish to be fulfilled.

Here is my favorite definition of hope: Hope is a **present** reality of a **future** event. It is a confidence you have, a belief so strong that the future event is going to happen, that you are willing to change your present lifestyle because of this future happening.

A word that is closely associated with hope in the Bible is the word "promise." Let me give you a powerful spiritual exercise and assignment. Sit down sometime with a highlighter and go through the New Testament. Highlight every promise that you read. Every time you read a promise that God has made, you are filling up your spiritual "hope chest."

Think with me for a moment. When was the last time you heard a message on hope? What about a Sunday School lesson? When was the last time someone stood up in church and sang a song that was entirely about hope? Go to the Christian bookstore and look around. You will not see much written about it. Sometimes a ministry will use the word "hope" in its name; or it may be used in the title of a sermon or an article, but there is really not much teaching on it.

Do you know where you **can** find an abundance of teaching on hope? In the Bible! Before we discover what area of darkness is driven out by hope, let us do a crossreference from the Scriptures and see some things God says about it:

"That being justified by his grace, we should be made heirs according to the hope of eternal life" (Titus 3:7).

"But sanctify the Lord God in your hearts: and be

ready always to give an answer to every man that asketh you a reason of the hope that is in you with meekness and fear" (1 Peter 3:15).

"Be not a terror unto me: thou art my hope in the day of evil. Let them be confounded that persecute me, but let not me be confounded: let them be dismayed, but let not me be dismayed" (Jeremiah 17:17,18a).

"Be of good courage, and he shall strengthen your heart, all ye that hope in the Lord" (Psalms 31:24).

"… which is Christ in you, the hope of glory" (Colossians 1:27b).

"Hope deferred maketh the heart sick" (Proverbs 13:12a).

"That by two immutable things, in which it was impossible for God to lie, we might have a strong consolation, who have fled for refuge to lay hold upon the hope set before us: Which hope we have as an anchor of the soul, both sure and steadfast, and which entereth into that within the veil" (Hebrews 6:18,19).

Note the wonderful line in that last verse: "Which hope we have as an anchor of the soul." What does an anchor do? It keeps the boat from drifting. What does hope do? It keeps your soul from drifting! But, it must be anchored to something solid and steadfast.

Once again, let us leave the abstract and go to a more literal level.

Captain Joseph Hartman was excited. He had been at sea with his first-mate and two helmsmen for nearly three months; their journey was almost over.

His trusty vessel, Scotty, was showing signs of wear, and his crew was eager to rediscover their landlegs. Hartman, however, was only excited about what the next day would hold. He was to propose to the woman who had driven him to sail halfway around the world: his dear Roberta.

As he surveyed the land that was barely in sight through the evening fog, he thought of the deadline she had given him... three months exactly. If he were to miss the deadline by even one day, she would be married to the man her parents had arranged for her to marry: a cruel, wealthy landowner who abused the peasants in her little Peruvian village. But he had not missed the deadline, it would come with the next dawning of the sun. Tomorrow he would claim his sweetheart.

Hartman looked up at the dark, threatening clouds; the storm was going to be a big one. He ordered his first mate, Dennis, to make sure the anchor was secure, and then retired to his cabin.

Throughout the windy, storm-tossed night, he dreamed of the life that he and Roberta would share. For the first time, he would have a home.

The next morning was bright with sunshine and redolent with fresh, after-storm smells.

Hartman came up from his cabin and stared blankly out at the nothingness surrounding the boat. Where was the land? Where was his Roberta? When he checked coordinates with Dennis, he found that they had drifted more than one hundred miles while they slept.

"I told you to secure the anchor!" he roared at his first-mate.

"I did," a nervous Dennis stammered, "I threw it overboard before I turned in."

Hartman raced to starboard and saw that although the anchor had been thrown overboard, the metal spool was still coiled tightly with rope. He angrily turned the crank and pulled up the anchor, which had been free-floating only six feet under the surface.

He had missed his chance for happiness, because the anchor, although lowered, had not been anchored on the floor of the sea.

This is exactly what happens in the Christian's life! We know the truth, but we do not anchor ourselves in it—it is not the anchor of our souls! We usually throw our anchors out, but we do not make sure they are gripping the Solid Rock. I'm sure you've heard the old song:

This rock is Jesus,
Yes, He's the One.
This rock is Jesus,
The only One.
Be very sure,
Be very sure,
Your anchor holds,
and grips the Solid Rock.

Once again, we must use our **spiritual preventive maintenance**. We must renew daily our hope in the Lord, and make sure that it is the anchor of our soul.

If we are not presently living with the confidence of Christ's return, and our eternity in Heaven, with what are we living? What do you think about during your day-to-day life? Are you living on a plane that tells you things are going to be okay because of the lifestyle you are leading? Are you dwelling on what the latest self-help author taught you? Are you giving credence to what a friend has told you about some kind of meditation or self-healing? Are you finding yourself just a little bit drawn to what you are seeing in the "New Age" movement?

No wonder Christians are so confused! Do you know what confusion is? It is **drifting** from place to place, idea to idea. Our lives must be based on what God tells us to do, knowing that the future will be okay, because we have built ourselves on the promises of the Word of God.

Look deep into your soul and answer this question: Do you believe, absolutely and with all of your heart, that Jesus is coming again? We are living in the greatest age of technology ever known. With all we can do through computers and satellites, and in the medical field, it sounds almost foolish to say you believe that Jesus is coming back and the rapture will happen just like the Bible says it will.

Do you really believe it? Not just on Sunday when you are at church, but on Monday and Tuesday, all through the week — at work, school, and home? Do you believe it? If you do, then you are experiencing the present reality of a future event. How do you know it is true? Because God says so in His Word.

That's why 1 Peter 3:15 says that we must "...be ready always to give an answer to every man that asketh you a reason of the hope that is in you..." A person can be born again and hardly ever read the Bible. On what will he base his reason for the hope inside him?

Just as an increase in faith is based on reading the Bible, so is the security of hope. Every single word in the Bible is inspired by God. I even believe that God inspired the covers to keep the contents clean!

Here's an even more unsettling question for you: If you do believe absolutely and without a doubt, that Jesus is coming back, will it change your lifestyle today? It should.

The Bible says that one of the five crowns given to Christians at the Judgment Seat of Christ is the "...crown of righteousness...," which is given to "...all them also that love his appearing" (2 Timothy 4:8). God is giving a crown in Heaven based on the hope we have on earth!

What if we were to hear a precursor, or warning, before the trumpet? Suppose a loud voice came from Heaven within the next few moments and proclaimed, "The trumpet will sound at nine o'clock tonight!" Would you still sit and watch soap operas? Would you watch the playoffs or the World Series instead of going out on visitation?

Remember, hope is a **present reality** of a future event and it is to anchor our souls firmly in the promises of God. It is a belief so strong that we are willing to change our lifestyles **today**, based on what we know God is going to do **tomorrow**!

Should this affect your decisions in day-to-day living? Of course!

Pretend there are two men standing in front of you right now. There is Bob on the left; he is what we call an unsaved "good" man. He is raising wonderful children, is actively involved in the community, coaches Little League, manages his finances, and is a great husband.

Sam is on the right; he is an average born again Christian. He also cares about his family, and is doing his best for them.

If Bob has a decision to make, here is the usual process: he gathers all possible data, considers the information, and makes his decision in light of what is best for him, his family, the people he loves, and the goals he has set.

If Sam has a decision to make, here is his usual routine: he gathers all possible data, considers the information, and makes his decision in light of what is best for him, his family, the people he loves, and the goals he has set.

"Wait a moment!" you are saying, "They're following the same process." That is true, and it is because most Christians only consider those areas when making a decision. Don't get me wrong, all of that should be considered. But there should be a major difference: Sam's decisions must ultimately be based on the teaching of the Word of God.

Here is where the necessity of Bible reading once more comes into play. How can Sam make a decision concerning his family if he does not know what God says about the family? How can he make a financial decision if he does not know that God covers finances in the Bible? This is true of relationships, time management, and any other important area. The Word of God is what firmly anchors our souls with hope, keeping us from drifting.

Now you have seen how necessary hope is in the Christian's life. You have learned that it will anchor you and keep you from drifting. But what area of darkness will the light of hope drive out in your life?

Galatians 6:9 says, "And let us not be weary in well doing: for in due season we shall reap, if we faint not."

When we have faith, we fear not. When we have hope, we "faint not."

What is fainting? It is that ugly word "quitting." What happens when we keep quitting? We get discouraged, and that is what we will cover in the next chapter.

Right now, however, before reading any further, will you look deep into your heart with your mind's eye? Find that rusty light switch with the word H-O-P-E written on it. Reach out and flip that switch to "ON!"

Get alone with God and say, "Lord, I believe your promises. I want my soul to be firmly anchored in the hope of your second coming. I don't want to drift around in confusion, miss out on the joy of victory, and end up quitting. I want the hope that is offered to me: I want to be anchored firmly in Your Word."

Other men see only a hopeless end, but the Christian rejoices in an endless hope!

HOPE

Psalm 43:5
"Why art thou cast down, O my soul? And why art thou disquieted within me? Hope in God: for I shall yet praise him, who is the health of my countenance, and my God."

Psalm 71:5
"For thou art my hope, O Lord God: thou art my trust from my youth."

Psalm 71:14
"But I will hope continually, and will yet praise thee more and more."

Chapter Five

The Step Through Discouragement

*Discouragement is
dissatisfaction with the past,
distaste for the present,
and distrust of the future.*
- William A. Ward

Let's talk about how it feels to faint. When my children were in their pre-adolescent years, attending our Christian school in South Carolina, it became all the rage with the students at one point to make themselves faint.

Here is how it worked: One of the kids would lean over, put his hands on his knees, and begin breathing very deep and fast for about 45 seconds. At this point he would stand, cross his arms over his chest, and hold his breath.

The person standing behind the "faintee" would immediately wrap his arms around his chest and squeeze, causing him to literally collapse on the floor in a dead faint! Isn't that lovely?

We were appalled when we discovered the practice and put a stop to it with disciplinary measures accompanied by lectures on the danger of cutting off the oxygen supply to one's brain!

Yet, in our spiritual lives we seem to "make ourselves faint" continually. We try to do something for God, we fail, we faint (or quit), and then what happens? **We get discouraged**.

I doubt that there is anything worse than discouragement. You have heard it called by different names, but it's

51

all the same thing. Whether it's the "blahs" or the "blues," whether someone's in a "bad mood," or in a "slump," or caught in a "rut"—it's all discouragement. You know what else? It is hard to have victory over discouragement, because discouragement usually stems from our own actions, even though we sometimes blame others.

Webster's defines discouragement as a deprivation of "confidence, hope, or spirit." Wow!

We have already learned that hope is having confidence that a wish or desire will be fulfilled, so what do you think happens, ultimately, when we have no hope? **We get discouraged**!

When a Christian faints, it means he begins well in really living for Christ, and then he quits. It may not matter why he quits, but the very act of quitting causes him to become discouraged.

I am sure you have come to the end of a year, when everyone is talking about New Year's resolutions, and said to yourself, "Good grief! I started out this past year to do this, and to do that, but I failed. I have failed God in this area, I failed my family in this area, I failed myself in this area." That is where discouragement comes in!

Discouragement is a by-product of fainting. It is going to be the next step—it is inevitable. We like the word "discouragement" because it fits right into today's cultural practice of labeling everything. But, let's face it, we are discouraged because we are defeated (now there's a word society does not like). We are defeated because we "faint" every time we start. We get started right, but we do not finish right.

We even make the right initial decisions, but we do not follow through by anchoring ourselves soundly in the Word of God and His promises!

I want to challenge your life through this chapter. I want you to be able to conquer discouragement, I long for you to experience the positive victory that is already yours through Christ!

Doesn't this prospect excite you? It means that, as a

child of God, you do not have to "faint;" you do not have to "be weary in well doing." You CAN fulfill the promise of the Old Testament prophet, Isaiah, who said, "...they shall mount up with wings as eagles; they shall run, and not be weary; and they shall walk, and not faint" (Isaiah 40:31).

Do you know what the first part of that verse says? Who is Isaiah talking about? He is talking about "...they that wait upon the Lord..." He is talking about the believers who live anchored to the hope of Christ's second coming! It's that simple.

I want you to read, and take to heart, what Isaiah tells us about the strength of our God in this chapter:

"Hast thou not known? hast thou not heard, that the everlasting God, the Lord, the Creator of the ends of the earth, fainteth not, neither is weary? there is no searching of his understanding.

"He giveth power to the faint; and to them that have no might he increaseth strength" (Isaiah 40:28,29).

How do you keep from becoming discouraged? You must keep your eyes on what Christ has done for you in the past, what He does for you in the present, and what he will do for you in the future! Hebrews 12:3 says for us to "consider him that endured such contradiction of sinners against himself, lest ye be wearied and faint in your minds." Do you think God is concerned about us quitting? Yes!

When you quit, or fail, do you know what happens in one split second? The devil rings your bell! "Hey, you really are no good, are you? You can't even do that little job; how are you ever going to do anything meaningful with your life? Those other people are so much stronger than you, that is why they can do it. You are just not cut out for this kind of life."

How can he do that? How can he get by with lying to us like that, when the Bible says, "Ye are of God, little children, and have overcome them: because greater is he that is in you, than he that is in the world" (1 John 4:4)?

The reason that Satan can lie to us, and get away with

it, is because we are living in the darkness of fainting, instead of continually turning on that light switch of hope!

Remember, we do not have to fight the darkness in order to get rid of it; we turn on the light and simply let it get rid of the darkness.

You do not have to understand discouragement in order to conquer it; let the light of hope do that.

Recently, I was on an airplane on my way to a crusade, when the two men behind me struck up a conversation. The younger man was talking about the pressures of his job and finances, and he said to the other man, who was considerably older, "I don't know, haven't you ever just been in a slump?"

"Oh, no," replied the older gentleman, "I'm much too busy for that." I loved it!

You don't have to attend a seminar, or take a psychology class to understand discouragement; you make a decision that you refuse to be discouraged. Is that too simple for you? Remember our human tendency to over complicate things, actually it is easy to do.

Your assignment for this week is to memorize Galatians 6:9. This verse will encourage you every time you need a lift. "And let us not be weary in well doing: for in due season we shall reap, if we faint not."

What does it mean to be "weary in well doing?" Simply put, it is when you say to yourself, "I am tired of doing this, it is never going to pay off."

What is "well doing?" Is it going out on visitation? Yes. Is it consistent Bible reading and prayer? Yes. Is it being faithful to your church? Yes.

But it is a whole lot more than that. What about doing the laundry? Is that well doing? Is doing the dishes after dinner well doing? What about cleaning the bathroom?

The reason we get so tired of well doing, usually, is because we do not even realize it is well doing! The devil comes along again and says, "Why are you doing those dishes? You know it's never ending. Why are you getting up every morning at the crack of dawn and going to work? You are nothing but a slave to this and a slave to that."

The culture in which we live will tell our ladies that they do not need to be good mothers, that it locks them into something that limits them. If they want to take care of their homes, prepare good meals, clean, and take care of the mundane details, they are not living up to their potential. That is so untrue!

We need to have our thinking transformed by turning on the light of hope. We ought to be saying, "Glory to God! I have this privilege of working towards a purpose in my life. Everything I do that brings me closer to the goal of raising my children to be good, Christian, happy, productive adults is the best thing I can ever do!" This is welldoing.

The Bible says, "But if any man provide not for his own, and specially for those of his own house, he hath denied the faith, and is worse than an infidel" (I Timothy 5:8). I do not believe it could be said any clearer. So when you are up and on your way to work, you ought to be saying, "Thank you Lord, for this privilege of providing for my family."

Here it is, this may shock you: **It can be just as spiritual for you to get up and go to work as it is to read your Bible**. It is!

You know what else? **It can be just as spiritual for you to wash, fold, and put away your family's laundry as it is to pray**.

Are you shocked? It is not the same activity, but since when does God let us choose which of his mandates we want to obey with enthusiasm and which ones we don't? We should be getting out of bed every morning saying, "Good morning Lord! I'm reporting for duty."

Colossians 3:23,24 says, "And whatsoever ye do, do it heartily, as to the Lord, and not unto men; Knowing that of the Lord ye shall receive the reward of the inheritance: for ye serve the Lord Christ."

God knew that we would grow tired of what we consider mundane things, He knew we would need a constant reminder!

What is our verse in Galatians talking about when it says "in due season?" Most of us want to reap on our schedule, and not on God's schedule. It is like that bumper sticker that says, "Lord, give me patience and I want it **right now**!" We have a way of praying, "God, could you please come down and bless what I am doing," when we ought to be praying, "God, would you please help me to be able to do what you have come down to do, in me and through me, and on your schedule."

This attitude adjustment makes a world of difference. The one is you setting your own agenda, and quitting after your deadline is met with no pay-off, and the other is a choice we make to live according to God's agenda, knowing that we "will reap, if we faint not!"

Do you know why our average parents do not spend every possible moment with their children? Because they do not see it as profitable. They just do not see the big picture.

Why doesn't the average Christian teach a Sunday School class? Because he doesn't think it is profitable. Why doesn't he tithe every Sunday at church? He doesn't see any profit in tithing.

These are outward symptoms of a life that is not anchored in hope.

A preacher friend of mine told me a sad story about a young man in his church (we'll call him Robert).

Robert received Christ during a revival and became very active in the church. It seemed that he was successful at everything he tried. He graduated from high school and married his high school sweetheart. He secured a very good job, taught a Sunday School class, and settled down for the good life of raising his children in a Christian home, while God met his needs.

When his children were about nine and ten-years-old, Robert suddenly lost his job. It threw him for a loop. He started looking for something else right away. He could not find anything. His family started to experience financial hardship, and Robert became embarrassed at the church's love and giving to help them.

Not long after these things happened Robert quit the church. His wife came to see their pastor, and said that all Robert did was sit around the house. He no longer showed interest in his children, in her, or in the upkeep of the house.

Over a two-year period, their marriage fell apart, although she worked as hard as she could to save it. Robert divorced her, left her and the kids, and moved in with his mother on the outskirts of town. His wife kept the children in church, and worked to support them, but never seemed to lose the "shell-shocked" look in her eyes.

It is so sad for me to hear of a Christian who seems just fine as long as everything is going his way, yet cannot conquer the slightest bit of discouragement, when something goes wrong. Robert allowed it to take root and grow until it destroyed his life and his family.

I know you have heard this statement before, but it is still so true: bad things do happen to good people. Just ask Job! The bad things only crush us when we rely on ourselves to handle them.

If the truth be told, most Christians today have an inward, secret philosophy that says, "I can do this for myself, I don't need God." We don't say it out loud, but "actions speak louder than words." We tell God through our actions that we are going to choose what will bless our lives, and what will get us ahead. Of course, we make the provision that if we stump our toes and fall a little bit, we trust He will be there, because we will be sure and call on Him then.

Remember, you will reap, "in due season." If you bring your children up to be God-fearing: "...but bring them up in the nurture and admonition of the Lord" (Ephesians 6:4), it may sometimes seem that things will not turn out well with them, but keep on trusting God.

The Bible says, "Train up a child in the way he should go: and when he is old, he will not depart from it"

(Proverbs 22:6). What greater promise do you need?

I remember the first time I tithed. I was in Bible College, but I had not been brought up under any kind of Christian influence. My wife, June, was used to tithing because her family tithed regularly. After we married, one of the first things she asked me was when we were going to start tithing. "Honey," I said, "I'm going to Bible College."

I was only making between $30 and $35 a week. June and I were taking a full load of classes, trying to prepare for the ministry, and I was working every evening at a grocery store. It was all we could do to have a place to live and put food on the table, and here she was, expecting me to tithe!

Every time that offering plate came down our pew at church, I would watch it go by, thinking, "I need money more than that preacher does. Why is he asking me for money?"

Well, the Holy Spirit kept reminding me that it was not the preacher I was obeying, but God. I'll never forget that Sunday when I wrote out my first check for tithe to New Testament Baptist Church in Columbia, South Carolina in the amount of $3.22 (I figured it to the penny). I gritted my teeth and put the check in the plate when it came by.

Guess what my first thought was? No, it was not one of rejoicing. I thought, "There, now everyone can get off my back!" I didn't know at that time that God loves a cheerful giver.

Well, I had always heard testimonies from others who said that as soon as they got right with God financially, He started blessing. So, I got ready for those blessings. I went to work every day that week expecting a raise. I checked the mailbox every day for that check I was sure was coming from somewhere. I did not get a raise, and I did not get a check.

"God," I prayed, "You've let me down." I talked to June and we decided to be steadfast and wait on the Lord. You know what happened? God started blessing!

You do not want to be like the fellow who plants

tomatoes one day, and pulls the plants out of the ground in anger the following day, because there are no tomatoes yet.

You do have to plant. You have to work, but you also have to wait for the harvest.

I want you to quote Galatians 6:9 to yourself all day today, and all throughout this week. "And let us not be weary in well doing: for in due season we shall reap, if we faint not." If you do not understand this verse, you are going to walk around so discouraged you will not be able to see the workings of God in your life and in the lives of others. Your chin will hang so low it will look like you've been eating grits out of a Southern stove pipe!

All of this is based on using spiritual preventive maintenance to constantly renew your hope in the Lord. Make sure the light switch of hope stays on in your life. Look at the blessings God has given you; transform your thinking to the point where you see the VALUE in the things you accomplish every day.

Before reading any further, take time right now and talk to God. Tell Him you have determined to live firmly anchored in the hope of His Word, His promises, and His second coming. Ask Him to make you grateful for the privilege you have of touching other people's lives, and of working towards personal and family goals.

God has given us everything we need to live wonderful, fulfilled, happy lives. Isn't it time we live like we believe what He says?

"I can do all things through Christ which strengtheneth me" (Philippians 4:13).

LOVE

1 John 4:16

"And we have known and believed the love that God hath to us. God is love; and he that dwelleth in love dwelleth in God, and God in him."

Chapter Six

Stepping Into Love

Love will find a way.
Indifference only finds excuses.

Jesus said, "As the father hath sent me, so send I you." How would you have liked to have been there when Jesus walked this earth? How would you have liked to have sat in the crowded city square when Jesus preached? It would have been amazing to have your life personally touched by the Son of God.

There has never been a man who has loved like Jesus loved. There has never been a person on this earth who has influenced more people for Heaven.

There is a principle that we, as individual Christians, need to follow and portray, particularly in this culture: People do not care how much we know until they know how much we care.

Let us go back to our pivotal, foundational verse, 1 Corinthians 13:13. "And now abideth faith, hope, charity, these three; but the greatest of these is charity."

You've already learned that when the light switch of faith is turned on it will drive the darkness of fear out of your life, allowing you to step over the obstacles in your path.

You've seen that turning on the light switch of hope will completely abolish the darkness of fainting, and will allow you to conquer discouragement in your life by resting on God's promises.

Now we are at the final switch. It's the light switch of love. I believe this is the most exciting light you can ever turn on in your life, but it is also the hardest. It is a decision that must be renewed constantly, because having true love for others is not an automatic human trait.

Does that surprise you? It shouldn't.

In this day and age, it seems that Christians are busier tearing others down than loving them. Jesus said in John 13:35, "By this shall all men know that ye are my disciples, if ye have love one to another."

Have you heard the old song written from this wonderful verse? My daughter wrote a short story years ago about an old, gentle, cemetery caretaker who tended the graves of people who were cut off and judged by Christians because of their actions, people who never saw the love of God in anyone who touched their lives.

At the end of the story, the old man is walking slowly toward a new grave with bright, pink flowers in his hand. As he kneels, tears trickling down his face, he softly sings that song:

> *And they'll know we are Christians*
> *By our love, by our love.*
> *Yes, they'll know we are Christians*
> *By our love.*

Yes, it's sad, though it's true. The number one evidence of a Christian in this modern age should be the love that shines forth from that Christian!

Let us do a Bible cross-reference and find out what else God says about love:

"Hatred stirreth up strifes: but love covereth all sins" (Proverbs 10:12).

"Greater love hath no man than this, that a man lay down his life for his friends" (John 15:13).

"For the love of Christ constraineth us; because we thus judge, that if one died for all, then were all dead:" (2 Corinthians 5:14).

"Let brotherly love continue" (Hebrews 13:1).

"Beloved, let us love one another: for love is of God; and every one that loveth is born of God, and knoweth God. He that loveth not knoweth not God; for God is love" (1 John 4:7,8).

"By this we know that we love the children of God, when we love God, and keep his commandments" (1 John 5:2).

"A friend loveth at all times, ..." (Proverbs 17:17a).

"Owe no man any thing, but to love one another: for he that loveth another hath fulfilled the law" (Romans 13:8).

That last verse is one of my favorites, and I do not think God's commandment could be any clearer: "...he that loveth another hath fulfilled the law."

So, do you believe that God wants us to love each other? He commands it! He says in our verse in 1 Corinthians, "...the greatest of these is charity." He says in Colossians 3:14, "And above all these things put on charity, which is the bond of perfectness." Remember that in the Bible the word charity means the highest form of love.

Christ loved us and saved us so that we could live a life of love.

Remember, not one of us can ever be successful if we believe that all we have to do is get right with God one time. We must constantly practice our spiritual preventive maintenance. This is true especially when it comes to love.

The Bible says we are to, "Put on the whole armor of God, that ye may be able to stand against the wiles of the devil" (Ephesians 6:11). Do you think a soldier only arms himself once, and the armor lasts him through every battle for the rest of his life? Of course not! He must constantly keep arming himself, just as we must constantly renew the faith, hope, and love within us.

Love is a choice. Whether or not you will love is your decision. I'm not talking about a "choice" as society defines it today. "Choice" today is just another word for anarchy; it gives people the excuse to do anything that they want, this is all nicely veiled by the phrase "an intelligent choice."

I am talking about the same kind of choice you make when there is a problem in your marriage, or with your children, or with a brother, or sister, or friend. You choose to work it out; you decide that you love this person, and that is what really matters. Do you know that is exactly God's attitude toward us? And it should be our attitude toward everyone, not just toward our family and friends.

Love is not only a choice, it is a basic need. You cannot survive without the light of love in your life. No one can! What's more, you cannot grow without an outpouring of that love.

One spring, our four children decided to plant flowers in pots and baskets all over the yard. One of the containers they bought was a long, hard plastic planter with designs painted all over it.

They bought good soil and seeds, and began their project. Soon, we had sprouts in all of the pots, baskets, and planters. The kids watered and fertilized them faithfully and they flourished.

One day I happened to notice that the leaves were all yellow on the plants in the long, pretty planter. They had not experienced near the growth as had the others in the yard, and the soil looked like it had mildew all over the top of it, almost swamplike.

I mentioned it to my son, Jon, who said, "I know, Dad, we don't know what's wrong with that one. They're getting plenty of sunshine and water, but they're not growing."

I examined the planter more closely, then laughed, saying, "There aren't any drain holes in the bottom of this planter. There is nowhere for the water to go; it is just sitting there stagnant, and the roots of your plants are rotting!"

That was a gardening lesson for them, and it is a good lesson for us. If we constantly take God's love and blessings into our lives, and have nothing overflowing, or "draining," out to others, we will grow stagnant. We must let His love flow through us and on to others!

If you turn on the light switch of love in your heart and mind, what final area of darkness will be driven out by the light? God says in Psalms 37:1, "Fret not thyself because of evildoers, neither be thou envious against the workers of iniquity."

The light of faith causes us to "fear not." The light of hope causes us to "faint not." And now, the light of love will cause us to "fret not." The light of love drives out the darkness of fretting!

And what a wonderful illustration is given with this verse! "Fret not thyself because of evildoers,..." God knew that we would look around and say, "This guy over here drinks every Friday night, and this one over here runs around on his wife, and yet they both are doing better than I am." He even tells us not to be envious of these people that we, in our hearts, feel should be paying for their sin.

Our job is to love them! I know you have heard this quote, but I wonder if you have ever really thought about it: "Love the person, hate the sin."

"Oh," you may be saying, "You can't mean the homosexuals and the child molesters, and people like that." Yes, I do. Those people were born into the original sin of Adam and Eve just like you were; they made some very bad choices, but God can still gloriously save them. Are we higher or mightier than God, that we feel we can stand self-righteously above them?

Sin is black; it has no place in our lives and needs to be rejected, but the person needs to be saved. We must separate the sinner from the sin!

It's hard to do this, I won't lie to you; that is why I told you that this light switch of love would be the most difficult for you to turn on, and to keep turning on.

We look at a popular crowd in our society and think,

"Look at them. They are turning our world away from God. They are heading us down a path of immorality. Why isn't God doing anything to them? Why are they so much better off than I am? They even look happier."

God said don't be envious of them. Look at the next verse, Psalms 37:2 — "For they shall soon be cut down like the grass, and wither as the green herb." Once again, it is all in God's plan. He has everything under control and He commands us to "fret not," but to love one another.

Let's think about love for a moment. Have you ever sat down and looked up the definition in the dictionary? It is such a common, household word. We hear it all the time from the day we were born (well, hopefully we do).

If you did happen to look it up, you may have noticed that there are perhaps eighteen definitions, and that's only when it is used as a noun! The most specific definition seems to say that love is to have a "strong affection," or to have a "feeling of kindness or brotherhood toward others." Vague, isn't it? But really, what is love?

There are three points you must understand before we can go any further.

First of all, everyone in the entire world is born with a negative attitude. When the Bible says, "fret not," this is what it's saying, "stop all of the griping and complaining!"

Bob Jones, Sr., who founded that great school, Bob Jones University, used to stand up in chapel on the first day of classes every year. He would address the incoming freshmen saying, "At Bob Jones University, griping will not be tolerated. If you are going to gripe, you might as well pack your duds and leave." And he enforced it.

Do you like to be around someone who gripes and complains? Is it a joy to hear someone constantly putting other people down, running down the system or authority? It doesn't matter what is brought up, this person can find a critical word to say.

How do we know that everyone is born with a negative attitude? Because we are all born into sin. Negativity is sin. It is thrilling to realize that God can give us victory over a negative spirit. He can!

The next important point is this: Often our first thought about everything that ever happens is a negative thought. Think about it for a moment. We might not say what comes to mind (thank God), but it does come to mind.

Take, for instance, the guy who just bought a beautiful, brand new car. He shows it to his neighbor, and the neighbor smiles a sort of plastic smile as he walks around the car.

You might say, "Oh, he's walking around the car admiring it." No, I can guarantee you that he is walking around the car trying to find something wrong with it! He can't help it, he's human! Envy is a human trait!

If he can't find a single thing wrong with it, guess what his first question will be? "How much did you pay for it?" And it doesn't matter how much he paid for the car, this guy can always get it cheaper.

I have a little rule: If I go out and shop around and buy something, and think that I did pretty well, and you could have gotten it for less, don't tell me! Let me think I got a good deal.

I have joked for years that one day I'm going to bring a message in a church on the one gift that most Christians seem to think they have, and it is not even listed in the Bible with the gifts. You know what it is? It is the gift of "inspection!"

Let's say I was able to meet you, face-to-face, at a crusade I was holding, and we conversed for a few moments. I am going to like you until I have found something wrong with you, then I will go around the church, telling everyone what is wrong with you. "It's just so they can pray." That just sounds so spiritual, doesn't it?

This situation would not transpire, of course, but I know you've seen it happen before. Maybe it has even happened to you.

Not only are we born with a negative attitude, not only is our first thought about everything normally a negative thought, but there is one final point that we need to understand. It is this: There is always something wrong with everything!

You know the only thing in this world that has nothing wrong with it? The Word of God! Do you know why? Because man did not do it! Anything that man has a part in will be flawed. It is inevitable.

Have you made a mistake since you accepted Christ? We all have.

So why do we not cease worrying and fretting about the things that are wrong, **that are going to be wrong anyway**, and then determine that we will live in the light of love!

You know what love is? It is the one emotion known to man that allows us to have a tiny glimpse of what it would be like if we did not have our human shortcomings. It is forgiveness, it is compassion, it is generosity, it is kindness, and it is so much more! That's why the Bible says that "God is love."

Let's look at a passage which covers the many functions of this one emotion (we will replace the word "charity" with love):

"Though I speak with the tongues of men and of angels, and have not love, I am become as sounding brass, or a tinkling cymbal.

"And though I have the gift of prophecy, and understand all mysteries, and all knowledge; and though I have all faith, so that I could remove mountains, and have not love, I am nothing.

"And though I bestow all my goods to feed the poor, and though I give my body to be burned, and have not love, it profiteth me nothing.

"Love suffereth long, and is kind; love envieth not; love vaunteth not itself, is not puffed up,

"Doth not behave itself unseemly, seeketh not her own, is not easily provoked, thinketh no evil;

"Rejoiceth not in iniquity, but rejoiceth in the truth;

"Beareth all things, believeth all things, hopeth all things, endureth all things.

"Love never faileth: but whether there be prophecies, they shall fail; whether there be tongues, they shall cease; whether there be knowledge, it shall vanish away" (1 Corinthians 13:1-8).

Do you need to look any further to see how God feels about love and how important it is to a Christian's life and walk with the Lord? This passage is taken from what is commonly called the "love chapter." I use it religiously when counseling a couple who will soon be marrying.

So, here's the normal life cycle of a Christian who is not living in the light of God's love: He is born with a negative attitude, his first thought about everything is usually negative, and since there is something wrong with everything, he spends much of his entire life searching for what is wrong, and therefore, wastes his life and opportunity.

We have to experience a Biblical, mental change, to the point where we look at everything through eyes of love instead of eyes of criticism and negativity.

I'm reminded of a song one of the girls in our church sang for Word Of Life competition one summer (she won, by the way). I always loved the words:

Let me see this world, dear Lord,
Through Your eyes, when men
Mocked Your Holy Name.
When they beat You,
And spat upon You, Lord,
Let me love them,
As you loved them,
Just the same.
Let me kneel with You
In the garden.
Pierce my eyes
With tears of agony.
For if once, I could see this world
The way You see,
I just know, I'd serve You
More faithfully.

We have to love like God loved. We need to show an example of the love of God and let God love others through us.

Let me remind you once again: The people you see everyday—the people at work, in your community, at the convenience store, at school—do not care how much you know until they know how much you care. And it is going to take the love of God to do this.

I told you I was going to ask you to turn on three light switches, and I have. You've mentally turned on the lights of faith and hope, and you understand that it is a constant, daily process to renew and strengthen them.

I am going to ask you, right now, to close this book and get alone with God. Look into your heart until you find that switch, whether it's shiny and new, or rusty from disuse. Find the switch with L-O-V-E written on it, reach out, and turn it on.

Simply say to the Lord, "God, I am promising right now to walk in the light of Your love. I know that it is a conscious decision, and I am making it right now. I want to see my neighbors, my co-workers, my family, and even the people I pass on the street through Your eyes. I want to love them the way You love me, dear Lord, so that they will see You through me, and not a judgmental, critical spirit. Make me thankful every day for what You are doing in their lives, and give me the compassion and desire to help them find You."

Now, enjoy the "peace that passeth all understanding" as God's love flows through you!

LOVE

Joshua 1:9

"Have not I commanded thee? Be strong and of a good courage; be not afraid, neither be thou dismayed: for the LORD thy God is with thee whithersoever thou goest."

Chapter Seven

The Step Out of Insecurity

*A man needs self-acceptance
or he can't live with himself;
he needs self-criticism or others
can't live with him.*

To be insecure means to feel unsound, to lack self-confidence, or to be unstable. Basically, it will cause you to wobble in indecision. Are you in touch with that emotion? It is not a good feeling. No matter what you do, you just cannot feel safe. Why?

The Bible tells us in James 1:8 that, "A double-minded man is unstable in all his ways." What is double-mindedness? It is not being able to focus, having all of your energies and thoughts split and going in different directions. It is a confusion that is caused by a basic feeling of insecurity.

Now, where does this insecurity originate? It is a by-product of fretting. Just as not having victory over obstacles is a direct result of fear, and being discouraged is a direct result of fainting, so fretting about things will inevitably lead to insecurity.

You may feel insecure about your job, about your relationship, or about your position on the School Board, it doesn't matter, it all stems from a feeling of insecurity about yourself.

You know what else? You do not have to go to a psychiatrist, lie on his couch, and have him tell you, at $75 to $100 an hour, that you are insecure. You know if you are!

It affects everything you do!

So, what is the flip-side of insecurity? Self-esteem. Webster gives a great definition: Self esteem is "An attitude of acceptance, approval, and respect toward oneself, manifested by personal recognition of one's abilities and achievements, and an acknowledgment and acceptance of one's limitations."

I need to make an important distinction here. I am talking about self-esteem, not self-love. I do not believe the people of our culture have a problem with self-love! Self-love is defined as, "The inclination or desire to promote one's own interests or well-being." Can you see the difference?

Self-love is detrimental both to the individual, and to society as a whole. It is the reason why some of our parents today are so selfish, and why many of our young people are experimenting with anything that makes them "feel good."

Self-esteem does not always make you feel good. If you will notice in the definition, it is an inward recognition of what your talents and achievements are, but it is also the knowledge that you have limitations and what they are. It's knowing that you have areas in which you need improvement, but also knowing that this does not make you a bad or inferior person.

You know, I have always disliked the phrase "inferiority complex," probably because I suffered with it a bit as a young person. My father was an alcoholic. There were eight of us children and my mother had to work at a Chapstick factory to support us. I had to get a job at a grocery store when I was twelve.

We never knew when dad would come home, or what shape he would be in when he got there. Basically, we were considered "white trash," although anyone who knew my dear mother and saw how she kept the family together would have seen us as anything but that.

I did not like feeling that I just was not good enough. I did not like the voice that whispered to me, "Look at those other kids in your class. They live in nice houses. They don't have to meet their fathers at the end of the driveway when he comes home drunk, just to keep him from growling and griping at mom as soon as he comes through the door.

I am not relating these things to make you feel sorry for me. My father was gloriously saved the same year I was, when I was nineteen. It took a little time, but we established a wonderful relationship, which we maintained until he went to be with the Lord in 1983.

I am telling you this because I want you to understand that I know what it is like to feel like you are not good enough to succeed. When I read what adults are doing to our children today, it breaks my heart. Whether it is abuse, exploitation, molestation, or neglect, they are taking their futures away. I wish I could pick every one of these children up and take them somewhere safe, and teach them that they are loved, that they are worth everything to God!

Whether you are ten, twenty, forty, or sixty, your attitude toward yourself will affect what you are able to accomplish, not only in your spiritual life, but in every area!

I need to make one more distinction before we go on. Have you ever heard of an educational fad called "constructivism?" According to Tom Loveless, who is assistant professor of public policy at Harvard's John F. Kennedy School of Government, constructivism "....is the idea that learners construct their own knowledge, that they hang newly acquired knowledge on a scaffold of what they already know." Sounds good, doesn't it?

When one of my daughters was taking education courses in order to get certified to teach high school English, she was blown away by the way this educational philosophy was inserted into classroom lectures. Her professors were telling their students that there really was no wrong answer, there is always a subjective side.

Constructivism is also called "self-esteem education." That is the distinction I wanted to make. The reason this is so is because these educators think that they are giving students the self-esteem they need to succeed, when they refuse to hurt their feelings by telling them, when they answer a question in class, **that they are wrong**. Now a teacher is taught to respond with, "That's very interesting, Johnny. You certainly are thinking."

These students are not gaining self-esteem; they are gaining self-love and self-importance. They are not learning how to cope with life. They are getting an exaggerated "sense of self" that does nothing to help them in the future. What happens when they get out in the real world and they make a mistake or fail at something? Do you think the supervisor at their job is going to walk on eggshells to keep their feelings from being hurt?

According to Loveless, who writes for *The Wall Street Journal*, "Schools have become institutions which exist primarily to nurture good feelings." What happened to feeling good when we work hard and succeed?

So, we have established that we are not talking about self-love or self-importance. We are talking about good old-fashioned self-esteem. But from whence does it come, and how do we get it?

I'll tell you, as long as you promise not to write me a letter and tell me my solutions are too easy! Here it is: Let the love of God flow through you to other people. Let it outpour toward others!

It is like this: Imagine a long line of people climbing a rope, trying to get over a wall. You are one of those people, and all of you are working together to succeed. Therefore, every time you can, you push the person above you, then reach down and pull the person below you a little bit higher. When you slow down and begin to feel a little weak, you feel a push from below, or maybe the person above you reaches down and pulls you up a little. That is the only way for mankind to succeed!

Here's a very important principle: If you spend your entire life pushing the people around you up, and reaching to pull people that are down back up, then for your entire life, you will experience people pulling you up and pushing you forward. But, if you spend your life putting down the people under you, and tearing down the people above you, then for your entire life, you will experience others pulling and tearing you down.

The very best exercise for strengthening the heart is reaching down and lifting people up!

You see, it is a matter of showing the love of God. That is the way to true self-esteem. Do you know why? Because when we let the love of God flow through us to others, it proves to others and to ourselves that we believe the love of God exists. What is more, it proves that we are worth something because God does love us!

Do you remember the little plaque from some years back? I bought one for my kids: "I know I'm something, 'cuz God don't make no junk!"

There's a children's song that the children's choir at church used to sing. I always loved the philosophy they were being taught when they learned it:

> *There really ought to be,*
> *A sign upon my heart:*
> *Don't judge me yet,*
> *I'm an unfinished part.*
> *But I'll be perfect just*
> *According to His plan,*
> *Fashioned by the Master's loving Hand.*
> *He's still working on me,*
> *To make me what I ought to be.*
> *It took Him just a week*
> *To make the moon and the stars,*
> *The sun and the earth*
> *And Jupiter and Mars.*
> *How loving and patient He must be,*
> *He's still working on me.*

He is working on us! It's time to take our eyes off of ourselves and put them on others.

My wife, June, is one of the greatest soul winners I know. She has such a loving, compassionate heart; she truly cares for others, and has a sensitivity to their needs.

Years ago when we were pastoring in South Carolina, we had a dear man named Millard who came to our church. He had been an officer in the army, and had just retired. He was very hardened and came to church only because his wife wanted him to go with her.

Millard would sit in the service, but he would not respond in any way to the invitation. I went to visit him and tried to deal with him. We had a good conversation, but I couldn't win him to Christ. Many people were praying for him, and his wife had just about lost hope. "Millard will never be saved," she told June and me sadly.

My wife became very burdened for Millard, and began to pray for him all the time. She went up to him at church one Sunday, looked him right in the eye and said, "Listen, I just want you to know I care." Then she continued to pray.

Two weeks later, Millard approached her after church and said, "Could you talk to me about getting saved?" She sat down and presented the Gospel to him. In a matter of minutes, that man got down on his knees and received Christ as Savior! People can resist anything but love.

Now, do you think June was battling thoughts of insecurity at that time? No, she was too busy letting the love of God flow through her and reach that precious man! That's what I am talking about!

This is what we need in our homes. The self-esteem of the man in that home is determined by the esteem he gives his family, and vice-versa. Try it!

Take for example, the dear wife, who nowadays usually has to work a full or part-time job, as well as take care of the home. Let us say she is home preparing dinner, doing laundry, cleaning a little, and taking care of the kids. She checks the time and stops to fix herself up, because her husband is due home from work at any time.

All of a sudden, in walks her husband. He doesn't kiss her hello. He doesn't tell her he missed her, or that he loves her. He sits down at the dinner table and begins inspecting.

He keeps on inspecting as she tells him about her busy day, then interrupts her to point at a tiny cobweb in the corner and say something sarcastic like, "I guess you were too busy to take care of that, huh?" With that one comment, he shoots her straight down in a heartbeat.

Now, why did he want to hurt her? Was he really all that concerned about a cobweb? Of course not. He feels like he is not good enough because she had to go to work. On top of working, she is managing the home just fine, making her look even stronger. His feelings of inadequacy keep building, until they come out in sarcastic little remarks that are aimed right at soft spots like cleaning, or disciplining the children, or something else.

What if he determined to take the attitude that he was proud of her for all she accomplished? What if he took his eyes off of himself and noticed how hard she was working and how tired she looked? Through loving her because of her commitment to the goals they have for their family, he restores faith in himself. He can accept the person he is and can understand his limitations. That is the only way our families are going to survive today!

Let's talk a little bit more about the love of God, and how it is all we need for security and self-esteem. Did you know there are dimensions in the love of God? There are.

• **Dimension #1** is the love of God for all mankind. One of the greatest expressions that you will ever read of that is John 3:16, "For God so loved the world, that he gave his only begotten Son, that whosoever believeth in him should not perish, but have everlasting life." That is the pivotal verse on God's love in the Bible. It has been a favorite of men since man began reading the Word of God; and no wonder!

John 3:16 shows the dimension of God's love — we call that an inexhaustible expression of the love of God.

• **Dimension #2** is the love of man for another man as the love of God flows through him. You see, I will never be able, in my own strength, to love my wife the way I should. I will never be able to love my children, my friends, and the people of this world the way I should, if I depend on my human capacity to love.

Human beings naturally center on themselves, and when you are centered on yourself, it becomes all you can see.

Dimension #2 can be divided into two expressions. The first is how we express ourselves to other believers, and the second is how we express ourselves to people who are unsaved.

As far as our expression to other believers is concerned, the Bible tells us "Bear ye one another's burdens, and so fulfill the law of Christ" (Galatians 6:2). It takes a great deal of patience to bear another person's burdens. You will never have this patience without the love of God.

Our mandate for our expression of love toward unbelievers is in Jude 22, which says, "And of some have compassion, making a difference:" We are to be weeping for the souls of lost people. How can we do that without the love of God?

The greatest expression of God's love through us to other Christians is when we bear each other's burdens. The greatest expression of God's love for the lost world is when we have compassion for them and win those lost souls to Jesus Christ.

These dimensions of God's love are higher than any one of us will ever understand. It is wider and deeper than our minds can comprehend. Very simply, God's love is an inexhaustible commodity which is available for us every minute of every day. You should be shouting for joy!

Let me tell you this: Until you can accept yourself, just as you are, as an object of the love of God, you are never going to experience the joy of God in your life, and you will never know victory. You must accept yourself as a creation of God! If you see limitations, surrender them to God. If you see exceptional ability, surrender it to God.

We will go even further: You must also accept other people just as they are. Don't ask any questions, just accept them. I don't mean go out and embrace people with habits that go against the teachings of the Bible, but stop fretting about them. Accept them as they are, and trust God for the rest.

You see, if God can love you in your condition, don't you think you could love them in their condition? God even has the upper hand; because He can see straight into your heart, every thought, every desire, every secret. You can not see like that into other people's hearts and minds.

Think that through for a moment. The kind of love God has for you will not happen in your love toward others unless you allow the Holy Spirit to teach you the tolerance and genuine love to do it.

It is called "unconditional love." It is the love a parent has for a child who keeps going astray. It is the love displayed by the prodigal son's father in that wonderful parable in the Bible (Luke 15).

When you get to the place where you are secure in the love of God, and you can love others through Him, wonderful things will begin to happen to you. It will begin to "leak" into all areas of your life, as you get a sense of your self-worth!

I am going to give you an assignment. God has given you a gift as a believer, but it may be sitting in a corner of your heart, rusty and misused. It's called the "gift of encouragement."

When you turn on that light switch of love, and it drives out the darkness of fretting, guess what happens? You stop all of the inspecting, and you begin encouraging others. Your goal, drive, and ambition as a Christian should not be to inspect, but to encourage! Isn't that wonderful? What a joy you'll be to be around!

One of the greatest encouragers I've known in my ministry was a deacon in our church in Michigan named John Carrel. I don't know the degree of his education, but he worked for the city of Grand Rapids. He and his wife, Geri, raised four boys. He coached Little League baseball for years and raised his boys to be real men. One of them is now a doctor, one of them pastors a church, one is an architect, and another of them is vice-president at General Motors.

John never missed a service. He was always out on soul winning visitation. I remember in those days after teaching Sunday School, that I would slip into my office to pray and get my mind focused on the morning message and the worship service.

Every time, without fail, I would start to walk out while the music was playing and the choir was singing, and there John would be. He would walk along beside me until I got to the steps of the platform. You know what he would say?

He would be so excited that his thumb would be sliding over his first two fingers in some kind of coaching signal as he encouraged me, "Preacher, I don't want you to get up there and just bunt the ball, I don't want a base hit. I want you to get up there and hit a home run! I'm not talking about an in-the-field home run. I want you to get up there and swing that Gospel bat and hit that ball over the fence, and get a grand slam for the glory of God!"

By the time I got up the steps and onto the platform, I would be busting at the seams! I would have to restrain myself to keep from going over to the music man leading the choir and shouting, "Sit down! I'm ready to preach!"

After church, when I would walk down the aisle so I could greet people at the door on their way out, guess who was the first person there to meet me! Brother John! He would say, "Preacher, you did it. You hit a grand slam! Don't you go home and think you can come back tonight and do any less."

The last time I saw John, when I was holding a crusade in Michigan, I asked him how much he would charge to travel with me to every meeting. Wouldn't you?

That is the gift of encouragement. I want you to work on that all this week; it will start to come natural to you in no time at all. Start complimenting the Sunday School teacher on his or her lesson. Tell your preacher that it was a great message (and stop tearing him down over the table at lunch).

Tell your wife that you just can't believe what she accomplishes in one day, and that you are so proud of her. Tell your husband how thankful you are to have a husband who is a provider and who loves his family. Tell the people at work that they are doing a wonderful job, and tell them often. Tell your children that you believe in them; tell them they can do or be anything through the power of God in their lives.

Do this for one week solid, then try to tell me that your concept of yourself has not changed. You will have the healthiest self-esteem on the block!

People do not need others reminding them of what they cannot do. They are already well aware of that, and if they forget, the devil is right there to remind them. People need to be reminded of what they can do, and you know what? They will do it!

That is what God's love will do through us.

Take a moment before going on and think about the three light switches you have now turned on in your life: the light switch of faith, the light switch of hope, and the light switch of love. Get alone with God. Ask Him to remind you to renew these commitments daily.

Work on encouraging others, and loving them just as they are while allowing them to grow. It is this process alone that will turn insecurity and unstableness in your life into focused, healthy self-esteem.

People sometimes succeed when others do not believe in them, but rarely does a person succeed if he does not believe in himself.

INVESTING
2 Peter 2:10, 11

"But chiefly them that walk after the flesh in the lust of uncleanness, and despise government. Presumptuous are they, self-willed, they are not afraid to speak evil of dignities. Whereas angels, which are greater in power and might, bring not railing accusation against them before the Lord."

Chapter Eight

Investing for Eternal Dividends

*It's funny how the value of man's riches
grows smaller each day,
while God's promises grow brighter and brighter.*

In the past seven chapters we have covered spiritual preventive maintenance, and how it can be used to keep the lights of faith, hope, and love continually on, in our hearts and lives. You have learned how to have victory over obstacles, and how to conquer discouragement and insecurity. Great! Wonderful! Now, you're all set to live a victorious Christian life, right?

By all accounts you are. But is that all there is? Do you want a little more? Perhaps you want to live a victorious and productive Christian life. Maybe you don't want to sit on the sidelines.

I remember when I had been a Christian for about five years. I was very happy in the Lord and felt I was a good Christian. Yet, I could not help asking myself, "So, what's the reason for all of this? What am I supposed to do now?"

The Lord showed me, through a series of events, something that forever changed my life. It put all of my commitments, trials, errors, accomplishments, and shortcomings into perspective. I learned that there is a purpose: I am supposed to be investing my life.

The dictionary defines invest as a verb: "To commit in order to gain profit or interest," or "To utilize for future benefit or advantage."

Basically, you need to think about everything you are

doing at this point. In what are you investing your life? Will it matter in twenty, forty, a hundred years? If it won't, then it's not what God calls eternal.

Two of the most powerful verses in the Bible are found in Mark 8:36,37. "For what shall it profit a man, if he shall gain the whole world, and lose his own soul? Or what shall a man give in exchange for his soul?"

I do not know of any particular passage in the Word of God that has ever challenged me more.

We have been laying the foundation for our victorious lives throughout this study. We have been asking God to help us understand victory. But why do we need victory?

Why is it so necessary to succeed in the Christian life? Why is it so important that we get to a place which allows us to experience both the joy and blessings of God, and the fruit we can bear in our lives?

Why are we stepping over the obstacles every day? Is there a reason that our faith is strengthened? Do we need hope just for a barrier to discouragement? Does love exist only to give us a sense of security?

We know we are to daily renew, through spiritual preventive maintenance, the faith, hope, and love in our hearts. We know that this will help us succeed in our family lives, in our relationships, and in our jobs. But is there anything higher?

There is something much, much higher. God wants us to be a blessing, first of all to Him, and secondly, to others.

When you accepted Christ as your Savior, you became a channel. You became a telephone wire, if you will, between this world and the next. Everything you do affects your efficiency and role as this channel. That is why you are reading this book. That is why you study the Bible and pray, and build your Godly home, and serve in your local church. It's because all of that makes you a more perfect instrument, and you can begin to invest.

God did not save us and leave us here on earth just so we could sit back and egotistically say, "Look at me, I have such joy and inner peace. I am probably the best Christian

I know."

God did save us and leave us here because He loves us and wants to bless our lives. He wants us to have success. He wants us to have victory. But, do you know what He wants more than anything else?

He wants people who will invest their lives for the future, not for monetary profit, but for eternal benefit. It doesn't matter how old they are when they start, or what physical condition they are in.

I think about Abraham and Sarah when they were elderly, and how God came to them and said, "I'm going to bless you with a child." What happened then? Sarah laughed. She said, "God, you can't do that. I'm too old." Within a year she was a mother. They appropriately named their son Isaac, which means "laughter!"

We, too, are incredulous at the promises of God. We say, "I don't make enough money to do that kind of thing," or, "I just do not have the sphere of influence that would take." Guess what? It is not you, IT'S GOD. It's not me, IT IS GOD.

If God can take something that has no potential and make it great, He gets the glory. He takes the insignificant, foolish things of this world, and He confounds the wise.

That's the principle we learn in 1 Corinthians, through the ministry of the Apostle Paul: "Where is the wise? where is the scribe? where is the disputer of this world? hath not God made foolish the wisdom of this world?... Because the foolishness of God is wiser than men; and the weakness of God is stronger than men" (1 Corinthians 1:20,25).

You see, if your life, your ministry, and what you do for God can be explained in human terms, then you probably did it. But if your life, your ministry, and what you do for God can only be explained in divine terms, then God did it, and God gets the glory! That is what He is looking for!

So, let us go back to our passage in Mark. Jesus is asking us what good it is for a man to gain the whole world and yet, in the end, lose his own soul.

Perhaps you're familiar with the story told in Luke 18 about the rich young ruler? This man came to Jesus and said, "How can I have eternal life?" Jesus told him he should be keeping the commandments, and the man said, "I've done that since I was a child."

Jesus then said, "Okay, but you are still missing something. Sell everything you own and give the money to the poor." Jesus knew that young man's heart! He knew he would turn away in sorrow, and not follow Him, because He knew that man had no understanding of God's riches or of real investment!

We can also learn from the parable Jesus gives us in Luke 12:16-21, called "The Parable of the Rich Fool."

> And he spake a parable unto them, saying, The ground of a certain rich man brought forth plentifully:
>
> And he thought within himself, saying, What shall I do, because I have no room where to bestow my fruits?
>
> And he said, This will I do: I will pull down my barns, and build greater; and there will I bestow all my fruits and my goods.
>
> And I will say to my soul, Soul, thou hast much goods laid up for many years; take thine ease, eat, drink, and be merry.
>
> But God said unto him, Thou fool, this night thy soul shall be required of thee: then whose shall those things be, which thou hast provided?
>
> So is he that layeth up treasure for himself, and is not rich toward God.

This is the story of a man whose soil was so good that it brought forth more than he could store. So he decided to tear down all of his barns and store all of his food and goods. Once that is done, he thought, he would say to his soul, "Soul, thou hast much goods laid up for many years; take thine ease, eat, drink, and be merry."

God answered him, "Thou fool, this night thy soul shall be required of thee:" Jesus made the analogy, and shared the moral of the story in verse 21: "So is he that layeth up treasure for himself, and is not rich toward God."

The Bible has much to say about the difference between earthly riches and eternal dividends. That is a subject very near to God's heart:

"Charge them that are rich in this world, that they be not high-minded, nor trust in uncertain riches, but in the living God, who giveth us richly all things to enjoy" (1 Timothy 6:17).

"Lo, this is the man that made not God his strength; but trusted in the abundance of his riches, and strengthened himself in his wickedness" (Psalms 52:7).

"Riches profit not in the day of wrath: but righteousness delivereth from death" (Proverbs 11:4).

"Thus saith the LORD, Let not the wise man glory in his wisdom, neither let the mighty man glory in his might, let not the rich man glory in his riches" (Jeremiah 9:23).

"That the trial of your faith, being much more precious than of gold that perisheth, though it be tried with fire, might be found unto praise and honour and glory at the appearing of Jesus Christ:" (1 Peter 1:7).

"He that loveth silver shall not be satisfied with silver; nor he that loveth abundance with increase: this is also vanity" (Ecclesiastes 5:10).

"Rejoice ye in that day, and leap for joy: for, behold, your reward is great in heaven:" (Luke 6:23a).

"Trust not in oppression, and become not vain in robbery: if riches increase, set not your heart upon them" (Psalms 62:10).

God does not mind us having wealth and security on earth. In fact, if we are disciplined with our money and budget, He will bless. But, you are not to set "your heart upon them." They will not last.

Let's look at the second question asked in our passage from Mark 8: "Or what shall a man give in exchange for his soul?" In other words, what are you trading your life for?

In Matthew 6:19-21, which is taken from the Sermon on the Mount, Jesus lays it out as plain as day for us:

"Lay not up for yourselves treasures upon earth, where moth and rust doth corrupt, and where thieves break through and steal:

"But lay up for yourselves treasures in heaven, where neither moth nor rust doth corrupt, and where thieves do not break through nor steal:

"For where your treasure is, there will your heart be also."

There is no way that Jesus' wonderful message about the permanence of what we accomplish for heaven could be said any clearer than that. What a truth for God to drive daily into your soul! "For where your treasure is, there will your heart be also."

I want you to do something right now. Put this book down for a moment and go get your checkbook.

Now, with your register open, I want you to scan down the last few pages, reading the names of the places to which, and the people to whom, you have written checks. That's the best "treasure meter" there is. Was most of your money spent on entertainment? I hate to be so blunt, but that is where your heart is.

God is teaching us, in these verses, how to invest our lives. He is giving the best time management seminar you could ever attend, and He does it in three verses! You've heard people say over and over how so-and-so needs to get his priorities right. Well, here is the way to do it.

Have you ever come to a point in your life when you

stopped and simply thought about what you were doing? Maybe you looked back and said something like, "I have lived twenty-four hours in the past day. At this same time tomorrow, I will have lived another twenty-four hours. God willing, by the end of this week, I will have lived one hundred and sixty-eight hours. Three hundred and sixty-five days from now I'll be another year older. What am I doing? Is any of this going to matter?"

Of course, as we have already covered, everything that you do to fulfill family goals and to raise your children right is eternal. Everything you do that touches the lives of your Christian brothers and sisters at church and in the community is eternal.

But, when it comes right down to it, if we are not pointing upwards toward heaven, and pointing that way for others, we are not investing for eternal dividends. And where eternal value is, that's where life really is.

Sometimes we Christians tend to think that when we start talking about Heaven, that we're talking about something that's just not practical. Let me tell you, in the midst of all of the confusion in this mortal world, Heaven is the only thing that really is practical.

> I counted dollars
> While God counted crosses.
> I counted gains
> While He counted losses.
> I counted my work
> By the things gained in store;
> But he sized me up
> By the scars that I bore.
> I coveted honors
> And sought for degrees;
> He wept and counted hours
> I'd spent on my knees.
> I never knew until one
> Day by the grave.
> How vain are the things

I'd spent my life to save.
I did not know until
Loved ones went above,
That richest is he who
Finds treasure in God's love.

I have preached message after message on this in crusades. I have said so often that one hundred years from now, you are not going to have the car you have now, your house may still be standing but it won't matter to you, your money will be spent, none of this will matter. It is nice to have these things, but get this: they are only by-products of the blessings of God.

He wants you to have joy in life and financial security. But you must make sure that you follow the stewardship plan God has left us. You must make sure that you have these possessions, that they don't have you.

Each of us has only three commodities to invest in our lives. You can collect every investment book, and every financial plan in the world, and study them until you know them backwards and forwards. It will not alter the fact that you have three, and only three, things you can possibly invest in.

Number one is your time, number two is your talent, and number three is your treasure. That's it. That is all you have.

That is why we have to reach a point where we are looking at what we have from God's standpoint. What can you do with each of them in order to reap eternal rewards? That is what Christian service, missions giving, and tithing is all about.

Several years ago, I came to a screeching halt in my life. It was May 13, 1976, my birthday, and I was thirty-five years old. I got up very early that morning and went for a drive. I was as near to being depressed as I had been in a long time. The thoughts coming to me were rather jumbled. They expressed feelings like, "This birthday sure crept up on me. How did I get another year older so quickly? I'm not ready for it."

Then, my thoughts turned even darker. I thought, "Man, if I die when I'm forty, I've only got five more years to live. Or, if I die when I'm forty-five, that's only ten more years."

I believe everyone has a time like this, and if you haven't, it is coming. It is the day you realize that you're not going to live forever. If Jesus tarries His coming and does not come in your lifetime, it's really not that long before you will be "...absent from the body, ... present with the Lord" (2 Corinthians 5:8).

Therefore, it will not be long before your investment will have already been deposited.

That day, my 35th birthday, I parked my car overlooking a beautiful, freshly plowed field, and I started asking God some questions. I asked, "God, as I search the Bible and read Your Word, is there anything in it that would show me that I have invested my life properly? How will I know?"

At that point, I had been preaching for more than ten years. I was pastoring a church I started in 1965. I was thankful for the numbers of people at the church, for the families that were restored, and for the growth we had experienced, but to be honest, I had never looked at it from the viewpoint I saw it from, that day in my car. I really did not know if I was investing my life wisely as far as God was concerned. I was not even sure I was "following the manual" correctly!

Why don't you ask yourself the same question? Let me phrase it a different way. If you were to die, and you looked back over your life, how would you finish this sentence: "I know I have been a success, because...?" Of course, I'm talking about the spiritual realm, not our limited, physical realm.

God tells us in 2 Peter what will happen to our physical realm: "But the day of the Lord will come as a thief in the night; in the which the heavens shall pass away with a great noise, and the elements shall melt with fervent heat, the earth also and the works that are therein shall be burned up" (II Peter 3:10).We brought nothing into this world, and we'll take nothing out.

After that long, soul-searching day in 1976, I began to diligently search through the Word of God, so I would know, once and for all, if I was truly investing my life for eternal dividends. After methodically combing through the Scriptures, I found that there are only two things in which you can literally invest your life and know that you have lived successfully (remember, I'm talking about "success" from a Biblical standpoint, which is knowing and doing the will of God).

Do you know what two things you can invest your life in and never lose? The first is the Word of God, and the second is the human soul. You search the Bible, and if you can find anything else that is eternal, write to me and tell me. I cannot find anything else.

So, in order to be successful, we have to invest our lives in what God says is important. This is the priority God has given us. He wants us to be the right kind of parent, the right kind of spouse, the right kind of citizen; He wants all of that and more for His children. He teaches us all through His Word how to carry out our responsibilities in these areas.

The first eternal investment, however, is in the Word of God. Let me promise you, if you spend your life in knowing the Word of God, you'll never lose it, and you will never be sorry.

That is why Bible reading is so vital! You have already learned that your faith, hope, and love cannot increase unless you are reading the Bible; now you know that every time you read it, you are making a deposit into an eternal investment.

We must realize the importance of the Word of God: "Heaven and earth shall pass away: but my words shall not pass away" (Mark 13:31). That verse shows the endurance of the Word.

"I will worship toward thy holy temple, and praise thy

name for thy loving-kindness and for thy truth: for thou hast magnified thy word above all thy name" (Psalms 138:2). This tells of the position of the Word of God.

"Wherewithal shall a young man cleanse his way? By taking heed thereto according to thy word" (Psalms 119:9). This verse shows the direction of the Word.

Finally, in II Timothy 3:16,17, we read of the necessity of the Word: "All scripture is given by inspiration of God, and is profitable for doctrine, for reproof, for correction, for instruction in righteousness: That the man of God may be perfect, thoroughly furnished unto all good works."

Blessed is the man who invests his life in putting the powerful Word of God into the lives of others!

Did you know it is not necessary for you to ever have to defend the Word? You do not have to be a scholar in the field of Apologetics. A soldier does not have to prove the existence of his sword or gun, neither does he have to explain why it is there, he just uses it. It is time to go on the offense with the Bible!

This Bible, written more than 4,000 years ago, contains 66 books which overlap and refer to each other without one mistake! Some mathematicians have tried to ascertain the chance of something like that happening accidentally, and they have come up with one trillionth to one chance of it happening! That is such a large number that we cannot fathom it.

Let's say you covered the entire state of Texas with a layer of dimes. Then you stacked another layer on top of that. Then you kept piling the dimes up, next to each other, until the stacks stood fifteen-feet high.

At this point, you have a helicopter fly overhead and drop a dime marked with a big red "X" in the middle somewhere, then set a blindfolded man loose on the edge of the state and told him to find that dime. The chance of him finding that one dime is the same chance there would be for the Bible to have all 66 books overlap, and support each other, even though they were written, through inspiration, by some 43 different men. The Bible is the Word of God!

Will you make a commitment to God right now that you will spend time every single day in His Word? Promise Him that you won't listen to the devil. Just remember, the devil only bothers people who are getting the job done.

If you do read your Bible faithfully, do you know what will happen? You will begin living and sharing the principles you have learned. It will overflow in your life, much like God's love overflows onto others! You will not only be able to tell people about God's plan or His grace, you will also be able to share the "why and the how," and not many people will listen to you without that.

The second area for eternal investment is the human soul. It is the time you spend sharing your faith with others and bringing them to Christ, and I believe it is the dearest thing to the heart of our Lord.

We will go into great detail on this in the next chapter, but I want you to get alone with God, right now, and ask Him to keep your heart open for what you will read.

Tell Him what you believe your priorities are, be honest and sincere about the changes you need to make in your life in order to invest in eternity. It will be worth it! Trust Him! "But as it is written, Eye hath not seen, nor ear heard, neither have entered into the heart of man, the things which God hath prepared for them that love him" (I Corinthians 2:9).

Prayerfully read over the words to this song by Keith Greene, a wonderful Christian songwriter who died in a plane crash in the early 80's. As you digest the wonderful dedication portrayed, vow to make it your prayer, as well:

> *Make my life*
> *A prayer to You;*
> *I want to do what you want me to.*
> *No empty words,*
> *And no white lies;*
> *No token prayers,*
> *No compromise.*
> *I want to shine*

The light You gave,
Through Your Son
You sent to save us
From ourselves,
And our despair,
It comforts me to know
You're really there.
So, I want to thank You now
For being faithful to me.
Oh, it's so hard to see,
When my eyes are on me.
I guess I'll have to trust,
And just believe what You say.
Oh, You're coming again,
Coming to take me away!

SERVICE

Psalm 37:3-6
"Trust in the LORD, and do good; so shalt thou dwell in the land, and verily thou shalt be fed. Delight thyself also in the LORD; and he shall give thee the desires of thine heart. Commit thy way unto the LORD; trust also in him; and he shall bring it to pass. And he shall bring forth thy righteousness as the light, and thy judgment as the noonday."

Proverbs 11:30
"The fruit of the righteous is a tree of life; and he that winneth souls is wise."

Chapter Nine

The Step Into Positive Service

Here's a three-word recipe for success:
Make Yourself Useful.

God did not save you to be a sensation.
He saved you to be a servant.

I am starting this chapter with one of my favorite success stories. It's the story of an amazing man named Jerry Traylor.

Many an endurance athlete tried but never completed a grueling 3,500-mile run across America. Jerry Traylor did. Many a marathoner never completed nearly three dozen of those 26-mile races. Jerry Traylor did. Many a strong competitor never had the strength to race three times to the 14,110-foot top of Pike's Peak. Jerry Traylor did.

And he did it all on crutches.

"But it's not the crutches, not the difficulty that matters," said Jerry. "What counts is the doing!"

Doing was essential to Jerry, of Parkersburg, West Virginia, who was 31 at the time he was interviewed. It was essential because during nearly half of his life, he'd been unable to do much of anything.

"For over fourteen years, I saw life pass me by," he said. "I was born with cerebral palsy and had more than a dozen corrective operations by the time I was in my early teens.

"You see," he continued, "There are two kinds of

crutches — positive and negative. Mine are positive crutches. They help me, support me, and allow me to get out and live life. But crutches can be negative, too, if people think that they are, and allow them to limit them or handicap them."

Jerry's crutches did not handicap him. He went to college, earned a degree in business administration, and landed a position with the Treasury Department. He also developed himself athletically and set about accomplishing increasingly difficult goals, such as running races on his crutches. Even so, Jerry felt compelled to do more.

He began running more marathons, and running them faster — setting an official record when he finished one 26-mile jaunt on crutches in just five hours and nine minutes. He went up against, and conquered, the steep, rocky heights of Pike's Peak, then repeated the feat the next year, and the next.

Finally, he undertook the biggest physical challenge of his life; to run across America. Starting from San Francisco late one February, Jerry followed a serpentine route he called "The Trail of New Beginnings" from coast to coast, arriving in New York City seven months and 3,500 miles later.

While people who thought he would never make it marveled at Jerry's extraordinary achievement, he said it represented no more than trying to reach his potential.

"I don't think anything I do is really that remarkable," he explained. "What's remarkable is life; that's totally remarkable. I think what I do is just live life and then make the best of every single thing the Lord has given me to use."

The focus of this chapter, our final chapter, is stepping into positive service. You have learned how to leave the negative aspects of life behind. Much of that is accomplished by being positive, by trusting, hoping, knowing, and loving.

You have learned that everything you do matters,

because you are making a deposit into some kind of investment, whether it be temporal or eternal.

Let us move now to what I believe is our number one
privilege as a Christian: the opportunity to share our faith
and invest in souls.

Remember, there are only two things in this entire
world that will reap eternal dividends if you invest in them;
they are the Word of God and the souls of men.

Simply put, we are to be putting what has happened
on our insides into action on the outside. We should be getting to know what God says in His Word, and sharing it
with others.

Before we go any further, however, I want to teach you
about the three adjustments that every healthy, producing
Christian must make before he can become that way. That
is all there are. Three. And, if you've made it this far in this
book, and have responded and made commitments at the
end of each chapter, then most likely, you have already
made two. Here it is, your plan for victory:

1) A Spiritual Adjustment. This is when a person
accepts Christ as Savior. It is the decision made in one's
heart and mind to receive God's gift of salvation, and to
become His child.

I hope and pray that you have made this decision in
your life; it is the most important decision that you'll ever
make. If you haven't, I urge you to take a moment and ask
Him to come into your heart. Tell him that you know you
are a sinner, and that He died to save you from your sin
and the penalty it brings. Tell Him you are receiving Him
as your Savior. He'll save you! Do you know how I know?
He said so in His Word!

2) A Mental Adjustment. This is what you have
been doing if you've been allowing God to teach you new
truths through this book. This is your decision to turn on
the light switch of faith, and the light switch of hope, and
the light switch of love in your life.

It is also your commitment to daily renew these, so that this faith, hope, and love will increase. It is your commitment to invest your life in eternal dividends, and to read the Bible in order to get to know God.

It is your decision to be a more consistent parent, so that your child will grow up understanding discipline; it is your firm resolve to be a better husband or wife, because you want the two of you to grow old together.

Basically, it is an assessment you make of your life, and a decision you make that the environment or family atmosphere of your background does not affect you today. This is so important! So many people are held back by the attitude that claims, "I can't help it, it's the way I was raised," or "My mom told me all my life that I was going to turn out like my dad. I guess I have." You must step away from that kind of thinking!

None of this will make you a Christian, but it will make you a better, and ultimately, a happier one.

3) A Physical Adjustment. I'll bet you can tell me what this is. It is walking what you talk. It is actually putting all of your mental processes, adjustments, and decisions into action. And I hate to break it to you, but all of the great decisions in the world will not turn you into a victorious, productive Christian if you do not follow through.

That is what we are doing here in chapter nine; I am urging you to begin right away, please don't put it off.

O.K., are you ready to take that step into positive service?

Investing in the souls of men... Doesn't that sound lofty? What is it? Is it teaching a Sunday School class? Yes. Is it working in the Youth Department? Yes, it is. It is going out on visitation, it is witnessing to others, it is inviting people to church, it is setting a good example for others so that they are pointed to Christ.

But, it is also cleaning the church bathrooms so that visitors are impressed and want to return, meaning they will hear the Gospel and God can touch their hearts. It is also working in the nursery so that parents will not be distracted from the conviction of the Holy Spirit. It is making a path for your Lord to work in their lives.

Have you ever taught a Sunday School class? If you haven't, I want to encourage you right now to ask God if He will let you. Go to your pastor and say, "Pastor, I would like to teach a Sunday School class."

The little bit of time that you will spend studying for the class, and the three or four hours a week that you spend visiting for that class (because every teacher must visit in order to see results) is worth it. The small amount of time for teacher training meetings, and the one hour you spend every Sunday morning teaching the class is worth it!

If you give yourself one year, if you spend an entire year teaching a Sunday School class, and don't let yourself get discouraged (remember our "hope" for the future!), you will never be sorry.

Do you know what you will do in that one year? You will influence a minimum of ten lives. When you influence those ten lives with the Gospel, you may not only be saving ten precious souls from an eternity in hell, but you will probably keep someone from getting a life-shattering divorce one day. You will probably keep someone else from a life of alcohol or drugs. Maybe you will even prevent someone from committing suicide.

You see, you need to see the big picture! Read the statistics! This is the way the Word of God abides, it is the only way. You can use your life to put the Word of God into others.

If God has ever touched your heart to go into the ministry, or full-time Christian service, or to teach His Word to hungry young people, do it! You will never lose your life, if it's invested in others.

If you are giving to missions projects, you are investing in something that will not ever fade. Your gift is allowing the Gospel to be spread world-wide.

When I was thirty-five years old, I made a decision

that my ministry would be based on nothing but revival and soul winning. You may wonder why I chose that dual theme. It's because "revival" speaks of investing our treasure and our talents, whatever God has given us, in getting out the Gospel. "Soul winning" is personally leading someone to the Lord, and training that person to do the same for others.

I have a good doctor friend who serves on our ministry board. Every time we get together for our annual board meetings, Richard will sit and listen for a few moments, then he will always interject, "What is the bottom line here?" I love that question. He wants to know how many people we had saved last year, and how many we are trying to reach through a current project! That is what is important.

Remember, the two things that will abide forever are the Word of God and the human soul.

We've covered the importance of the Word of God. Now, I want you to consider with me the human soul. Remember our verses from Mark — "For what shall it profit a man, if he shall gain the whole world, and lose his own soul? Or what shall a man give in exchange for his soul?"

What could we possibly get that is as valuable as the human soul? You see, there was a time when you did not exist, there was a time that you came into existence, but there will **never be a time when you cease to exist**!

Now, that cannot be said of Jesus Christ. In John 1:1, the Bible says, "In the beginning was the Word, and the Word was with God, and the Word was God." There was never a time when God did not exist, He's the Alpha and Omega, the beginning and the end.

But since God breathed, there in your mother's womb, and you became a living soul, you became immortal, and will never cease to exist.

It is like a watch in a case. The watch ticks, tells time, and is full of life. If you take the back off the case, then take the insides out and lay them to the side, you can sit there and stare at the case, but it won't do anything. It is empty. Maybe you would say, "This watch is dead."

You would feel bad, so you would want to give the watch a dignified burial. You can put it in a casket, hold a service, and bury it. But then you look over to the side and see those insides and realize that there is something — the life — that is living on! That's the way it is with the human soul.

We can bury the body, but the body is only the container of the person. The real person is the human soul.

What I am doing right now is trying to plant a seed in your mind. I am trying to get you to think about the immortality of everyone's soul, so that your priorities will have no trouble falling into place. When you invest in human things, you get human results, but when you invest your life in divine things, you get eternal results!

The Bible tells us that when we die, it is not really death, but simply "falling asleep." Back in Luke 8, in our story of Jairus from chapter two, Jesus told Jairus and his family after the maiden died, to "...Weep not; she is not dead, but sleepeth" (Luke 8:52).

God tells us in Daniel of the second coming, and how the souls of both the saved and the unsaved are eternal, "And many of them that sleep in the dust of the earth shall awake, some to everlasting life, and some to shame and everlasting contempt" (Daniel 12:2).

Why don't you think about that as you lay your head on your pillow and go to sleep tonight? Here is that "bottom line"— Heaven is eternal and hell is eternal.

That "sleep" when you lay your head down on the bosom of Christ because He says, "Come on home, I'm ready for you," is when your soul goes into the presence of God, and your body stays behind. It will be wonderful!

The Bible also tells us that the Lord is coming back "...with a shout, with the voice of the archangel, and with the trump of God: and the dead in Christ shall rise first: Then we which are alive and remain shall be caught up together with them in the clouds, to meet the Lord in the air: and so shall we ever be with the Lord" (1 Thessalonians 4:16,17). That is exciting! Thank God for salvation! Thank God for the rapture!

But there is a sad part to all of this. There are many, many people who have not been reached for Jesus Christ. They will know none of this joy, only sorrow and torment. If we have that light switch of love continually turned on, how can we let this happen?

In the Gospel of John, Jesus said, "Marvel not at this: for the hour is coming, in the which all that are in the graves shall hear his voice, And shall come forth; they that have done good, unto the resurrection of life; and they that have done evil, unto the resurrection of damnation" (John 5:28,29).

There will be two resurrections and two judgments, separated by a thousand years. Jesus told us there is to be a resurrection of life for the saved. This resurrection will be in two stages (I Cor. 15: 51-53). The first stage at the Rapture, the second stage at the close of the Tribulation (Revelation 20:1-6). Jesus also spoke of the resurrection of damnation for the lost who will stand before the Great White Throne (Rev. 20: 11-15). At that time, the lost will be judged and then consigned to the lake of fire forever.

You are asking me now, "Are you trying to scare me, or make me feel guilty?" I wish that I could! Do you think you'll be scared at the Great White Throne Judgment? Do you think you will feel guilty when you are standing in Heaven, and you have to watch a son or daughter being told by our Heavenly Father, "Depart from me, I never knew you," and then being pulled, screaming, away from God, and thrown into the Lake of Fire by the angels?

What about the grocery store cashier you have known for years? She is that sweet lady who always wants to know how you are doing, how the kids are, and whether or not you think it will rain. Will you feel guilty when she turns to look into the crowd and sees you standing there, ready to enter into "the joy of the Lord?" Maybe she will point her finger at you and say, "I saw you all the time! We talked to each other! You knew this was coming, yet you never told me!"

The Bible says there will be weeping in Heaven, and I believe all of us will cry when we see others being cast into the eternal lake of fire. But how much worse it will be if people that you see, people that you knew in life on earth, are people you never once told. That is what I am talking about when I say investing in the human soul reaps eternal dividends. God is saving them from hell through your witness!

The Bible also gives us a promise. After we have seen this, and suffered, "...God shall wipe away all tears from their eyes; and there shall be no more death, neither sorrow, nor crying, neither shall there be any more pain: for the former things are passed away" (Revelation 21:4). I believe that if God did not wipe away our tears, there is no way any of us could enjoy Heaven.

But the unsaved will not have their memories erased — they will live forever with the knowledge that they could have received Christ, and maybe they will remember their neighbor next door, the one their family barbecued with every week, who never once mentioned God.

I want you to think right now, has your mother been reached for Christ? Has your grandchild been reached for Christ? Has your co-worker, whom you have known for years, ever been told about what Christ did for him or her on the cross?

How valuable is the human soul to you? If you are saying, "I'm not really concerned about whether or not someone goes to hell, it's not really my concern," then you are dead wrong. You would be concerned if it were your dad. Well, if it is not your dad, it is probably someone's dad, someone's sister, someone's uncle. And every soul is equally precious to Christ.

A few months ago, our ministry missions team returned from the Philippines. It was our sixth crusade there. We saw, over a ten-day period, more than 1,200 precious people come forward and receive Christ. That is where the joy is!

There was one man who sat on the front row every night who had one of the hardest expressions on his face that I had ever seen. The people there speak a little English. There is really no language barrier in preaching as long as you keep it very simple. I knew he could understand the message.

That man sat there and smirked. He scowled at me, and smiled sarcastically when I spoke of God's love. But then he came back the next night and the next! He always sat in the same place, and I must admit I was puzzled.

On the third night, when I had everyone bow their heads for the invitation, I was watching him, and I was praying very hard. I watched his hands as they worked back and forth together, I watched as his shoulders began to shake a little, and I watched as he suddenly stood up, came forward, and received Christ as his Savior! There is nothing in this world that can match this.

After the service, I went up and introduced myself to him, and he was smiling from ear to ear. He told me he had been fighting God for years. Do you know what role I played in the destiny of this man's eternal soul? I was simply the channel, and God worked through me.

You see, that man is just as important to God as I am; he is just as important to God as you are. He's as important as anyone on this earth to our Savior, and one day I will see him again in Heaven! If that doesn't send shivers down your spine, I don't know what will.

Now, I want you to measure the value of one soul by the question asked by Jesus in Mark 8:36, "For what shall it profit a man, if he shall gain the whole world, and lose his own soul?" He is saying that the soul is worth more than the entire world!

In I John 2:15-17, Jesus says, "Love not the world, neither the things that are in the world. If any man love the world, the love of the Father is not in him. For all that is in the world, the lust of the flesh, and the lust of the eyes, and the pride of life, is not of the Father, but is of the world.

And the world passeth away, and the lust thereof: but he that doeth the will of God abideth forever."

Once again, I ask you, could the Bible be any clearer? What is this "lust of the flesh?" It is the consuming desire to do. What is this "lust of the eyes?" It is the consuming desire to have. What is this "pride of life?" It is simply the consuming desire to be.

If I could give you everything you have ever wanted, and let you do everything you have ever wanted to do — past, present, and future — and could make you into whatever person you want to be, even the president or a famous movie star, all of it could not equal the value of one person's soul!

Here is where you will step into service. If you do not understand the value of a soul, you may start teaching a Sunday School class, but you are not going to last long. You may take on a bus route, but you will quit when you hit the first obstacle, because you will not understand the value of that nine-year-old boy's soul. The boy you visit and bring to church is more important than any obstacle you may face.

His nose may run, and he may smell like he has not bathed in days, but he is as important as you are. So many churches today have this attitude that they want to clean people up before they bring them in. Let me ask you, does a fisherman clean the fish before he catches it? Did Jesus care if the person he won was dirty, or full of sin?

We don't get better to get saved, we get saved to get better. It is just that simple!

At the end of this book (Appendix A) you will find a thirteen-point soul winning plan that we have developed, as well as hints in using the plan effectively.

I am asking you to make a commitment and study this plan until you know it by heart. Use it to witness and share your faith with those on the job, with your neighbors, and with your family and friends. There is nothing greater or higher you can do with your life.

Well we have finished our study, and I have given you as practical a plan for victory in the Christian life as I believe can be found.

You have made several commitments as we went along:

1. You have turned on the light switch of faith in your life, understanding that this faith, daily renewed, will cause you to "fear not."

2. You have committed to using faith to conquer the obstacles you face, understanding that not defeating the obstacles is a direct result of fear.

3. You have turned on the light switch of hope in your life, understanding that this hope, daily renewed, will cause you to "faint not."

4. You have committed to trusting in the promises of God's Word and His return so that you will have victory over discouragement, which is a direct result of fainting.

5. You have turned on the light switch of love in your life, understanding that the love of God, pouring through you and onto others, will cause you to "fret not."

6. You have committed to loving others and letting God love them through you, therefore conquering all doubt and insecurity, because it is only through this love that you can find true self-esteem.

7. You have made a commitment to invest your life in what is eternal, and not in what is temporal.

8. You have made a commitment that you will invest yourself in the Word of God and the souls of men.

Get alone with God right now. Renew these commitments, and ask Him to help you as you follow this plan for victory. Get some real Christian friends to spend time with, Christians who want to invest their lives in the future. Surround yourself with friends who see the "big picture."

May God bless you as He gives you the joyous, victorious, productive life He has for you!

Appendix A

"Go ye therefore into all the world" A Step-By-Step Soul-Winning Plan

Getting on the Subject - Ask Him:
1. "What is your church background?" Now, give your salvation testimony.
2. "If you should die right now, are you sure that you would go to Heaven?"
3. "May I take a moment and show you how you can know for sure?"

Now, Teach Him from the Bible:
4. That all have sinned (Romans 3:23).
5. That the penalty of sin is death & hell (Romans 6:23).
6. That Jesus paid the penalty (Romans 5:8).
7. That if he will believe that and receive Christ, God will save him (Romans 10:13).

Now, Help Him to Receive Christ - Have Him:
8. Bow his head in prayer - you pray and ask God to help him be willing to receive Christ.
9. Pray aloud and receive Christ - lead him in a phrase-by-phrase sinners' prayer.
10. Take your hand if he meant business.
11. Now, you pray, thankful for his decision.

Now, Help Him Begin to Grow:
12. Give him assurance of salvation (Romans 10:13).

13. Lead him to make it public in the local church (Romans 10:11 & Matthew 10:32).

This plan has been designed to help you win your friends and family to Christ. The following will enable you to use it more effectively:

•   Read it over several times, with the verses, until you are thoroughly familiar with it.

•   Depend on the Holy Spirit's power as you present the plan.

•   Spend some time being friendly before starting at step #1.

•   After starting the plan, don't get off the track on a side issue.

•   Never put the person down — don't criticize his background or religious affiliation.

•   Note that once his head is bowed at step #8, it remains bowed until the end of step #11.

•   Once he is saved, make sure you spend the time necessary to help him grow, get into a Bible-preaching church, and learn how to win his friends to Christ.

Plan developed by
Evangelist David A. Wood, D.D.
For more information on soul winning helps, write:
DAVID WOOD MINISTRIES
P.O. BOX 387
Trenton, GA 30752
Or call 706/657-6043

Appendix B

As You Step Into the Light

You have read the nine chapters on this book's theme. Many verses from the Word of God have been quoted. Now I want to ask you to read carefully and prayerfully the three great Bible chapters on Faith, Hope, and Love which follow.

Read them slowly and thoughtfully. Ask God to enable you to grasp the wonderful truth in these chapters. Ask the Holy Spirit to apply them to your life.

They are set forth differently than you would ordinarily find them in your Bible. Not a word has been altered here, but the arrangement is different.

Verse divisions are not included. Each passage can flow in a paragraph or in separate poetry-like lines for easy meditation.

The Faith chapter is printed in paragraphs with headings, mentioning the person or content of the passage. To Hebrews 11 are added the first two verses of chapter 12, making a complete Holy Spirit-inspired essay on Faith for your edification with an opening sentence and a grande finale, focusing on Jesus, the Author and Finisher of our Faith.

The Hope chapter, Romans 8, is arranged in poetic sentences with contrasting ideas and matching truths running parallel when possible. The stanzas include one or more standard verses and run from four lines to as many as seven or eight.

The Love chapter, 1 Corinthians 13, uses the word Love instead of Charity, since the latter word has somewhat changed in meaning since the Greek word *agape* was first translated into English by William Tyndale in 1525.

The word means the highest and purest form of Love.

I challenge you to read these three chapters every day for a month, asking God to lead you into the Light through His wonderful Word.

"Thy word is a lamp unto my feet and a light unto my path ..."

Appendix C

FAITH

The Honor Roll of Men and Women of Faith

Hebrews 11, 12:1,2
Pleasing God with Faith

Now FAITH is the substance of things hoped for, the evidence of things not seen. For by it the elders obtained a good report. Through FAITH we understand that the worlds were framed by the word of God, so that things which are seen were not made of things which do appear.

Abel

By FAITH Abel offered unto God a more excellent sacrifice than Cain, by which he obtained witness that he was righteous, God testifying of his gifts: and by it he being dead yet speaketh.

Enoch

By FAITH Enoch was translated that he should not see death; and was not found, because God had translated him: for before his translation he had this testimony, that he pleased God. But without FAITH it is impossible to please him: for he that cometh to God must believe that he is, and that he is a rewarder of them that diligently seek him.

Noah

By FAITH Noah, being warned of God of things not

seen as yet, moved with fear, prepared an ark to the saving of his house; by the which he condemned the world, and became heir of the righteousness which is by FAITH.

Abraham

By FAITH Abraham, when he was called to go out into a place which he should after receive for an inheritance, obeyed; and he went out, not knowing whither he went. By FAITH he sojourned in the land of promise, as in a strange country, dwelling in tabernacles with Isaac and Jacob, the heirs with him of the same promise: for he looked for a city which hath foundations, whose builder and maker is God.

Sara

Through FAITH also Sara herself received strength to conceive seed, and was delivered of a child when she was past age, because she judged him faithful who had promised. Therefore sprang there even of one, and him as good as dead, so many as the stars of the sky in multitude, and as the sand which is by the seashore innumerable.

These all died in FAITH, not having received the promises, but having seen them afar off, and were persuaded of them, and embraced them, and confessed that they were strangers and pilgrims on the earth. For they that say such things declare plainly that they seek a country. And truly, if they had been mindful of that country from whence they came out, they might have had opportunity to have returned. But now they desire a better country, that is, an heavenly: wherefore God is not ashamed to be called their God: for he hath prepared for them a city.

Abraham

By FAITH Abraham, when he was tried, offered up Isaac: and he that had received the promises offered up his only begotten son, of whom it was said, "In Isaac shall thy seed be called": accounting that God was able to raise him up, even from the dead; from whence also he received him in a figure.

Isaac

By FAITH Isaac blessed Jacob and Esau concerning things to come. By FAITH Jacob, when he was dying, blessed both the sons of Joseph; and worshiped, leaning upon the top of his staff.

Joseph

By FAITH Joseph, when he died, made mention of the departing of the children of Israel; and gave commandment concerning his bones.

Moses

By FAITH Moses, when he was born, was hid three months of his parents, because they saw he was a proper child; and they were not afraid of the king's commandment. By FAITH Moses, when he was come to years, refused to be called the son of Pharaoh's daughter; choosing rather to suffer affliction with the people of God, than to enjoy the pleasures of sin for a season; esteeming the reproach of Christ greater riches than the treasures in Egypt: for he had respect unto the recompense of the reward. By FAITH he forsook Egypt, not fearing the wrath of the king: for he endured, as seeing him who is invisible. Through FAITH he kept the passover, and the sprinkling of blood, lest he that destroyed the firstborn should touch them. By FAITH they passed through the Red Sea as by dry land: which the Egyptians assaying to do were drowned.

Joshua

By FAITH the walls of Jericho fell down, after they were compassed about seven days.

Rahab

By FAITH the harlot Rahab perished not with them that believed not, when she had received the spies with peace.

And Others

And others were tortured, not accepting deliverance; that they might obtain a better resurrection: and others had trial of cruel mockings and scourgings, yea, moreover of bonds and imprisonment: they were stoned, they were sawn asunder, were tempted, were slain with the sword: they wandered about in sheepskins and goatskins; being destitute, afflicted, tormented; (of whom the world was not worthy). They wandered in deserts, and in mountains, and in dens and caves of the earth. And these all, having obtained a good report through FAITH, received not the promise; God having provided some better thing for us, that they without us should not be made perfect.

The Author and Finisher of Our Faith

Wherefore seeing we also are compassed about with so great a cloud of witnesses, let us lay aside every weight, and the sin which doth so easily beset us, and let us run with patience the race that is set before us, looking unto Jesus, the author and finisher of our FAITH; who for the joy that was set before him endured the cross, despising the shame, and is set down at the right hand of the throne of God.

Appendix D

HOPE

Saved by Hope

Romans 8

There is therefore now no condemnation
    To them which are in Christ Jesus,
Who walk not after the flesh
    But after the Spirit.

For the law of the Spirit of life in Christ Jesus
    Hath made me free from the law of sin and death.
For what the law could not do in that it was weak through
    the flesh,
    God sending his own son in the likeness of sinful flesh,
And for sin, condemned sin in the flesh.

That the righteousness of the law might be fulfilled in us,
    Who walk not after the flesh, but after the Spirit.
For they that are after the flesh do mind the things of the
    flesh;
    But they that are after the Spirit, the things of the
Spirit.

For to be carnally minded is death,
    But to be spiritually minded is life and peace.
Because the carnal mind is enmity against God.
    For it is not subject to the law of God, neither indeed
can be.

So then they that are in the flesh cannot please God.
    But ye are not in the flesh, but in the Spirit,

If so be that the Spirit of God dwell in you.
    And if Christ be in you, the body is dead because of sin,
But the Spirit is life because of righteousness.

But if the spirit of him that raised up Jesus from the
    dead
Dwell in you, he that raised up Christ from the dead
Shall also quicken your mortal bodies
    By his Spirit that dwelleth in you.

Therefore we are debtors, not to the flesh,
    To live after the flesh.
For if ye live after the flesh, ye shall die:
    But if ye through the spirit
Do mortify the deeds of the body, ye shall live.

For as many as are led by the Spirit of God,
    They are the sons of God.
For ye have not received the spirit of bondage again to fear;
    But ye have received the Spirit of adoption,
Whereby we cry, "Abba, Father."

The Spirit itself beareth witness with our spirit,
    That we are the children of God: and if children,
Then heirs, heirs of God, and joint heirs with Christ;
    If so be that we suffer with him,
That we may be also glorified together.

For I reckon that the sufferings of this present time
    Are not worthy to be compared with the glory
That shall be revealed in us.

For the earnest expectation of the creature
    Waiteth for the manifestation of the sons of God.
For the creature was made subject to vanity, not
    willingly,
But by reason of him who hath subjected the same in
    HOPE,

Because the creature itself also shall be delivered
      From the bondage of corruption into the glorious
      liberty
Of the children of God.
      For we know that the whole creation groaneth and
      travaileth
In pain together until now.

And not only they, but ourselves also,
      Which have the first fruits of the Spirit, even we
Ourselves groan within ourselves, waiting for the adoption,
      To wit, the redemption of our body.

For we are saved by HOPE, but HOPE that is seen is not
      HOPE;
      For what a man seeth, why doth he yet HOPE for?
But if HOPE for that we see not,
      Then do we with patience wait for it.

Likewise the Spirit also helpeth our infirmities:
      For we know not what we should pray for as we ought:
But the Spirit itself maketh intercession of us
      With groanings which cannot be uttered.

And he that searcheth the hearts
      Knoweth what is the mind of the Spirit,
Because he maketh intercession for the saints
      According to the will of God.

And we know that all things work together for good
      To them that love God, to them who are the called
According to his purpose.

For whom he did foreknow, he also did predestinate
      To be conformed to the image of his Son,
That he might be the firstborn among many brethren.
      Moreover whom he did predestinate, them he also

called:
And whom he called, them he also justified:
    And whom he justified, them he also glorified.

What shall we then say to these things?
    If God be for us, who can be against us?
He that spared not his own Son, but delivered him up for
    us all,
    How shall he not with him also freely give us all
things?

Who shall lay anything to the charge of God's elect?
    It is God that justifieth.
Who is he that condemneth?
    It is Christ that died, yea rather, that is risen again,
Who is even at the right hand of God,
    Who also maketh intercession for us.

Who shall separate us from the love of Christ?
    Shall tribulation, or distress, or persecution
Or famine, or nakedness, or peril or sword? As it is written;
    "For thy sake we are killed all the day long;
We are accounted as sheep for the slaughter."

Nay, in all these things we are more than conquerors
    Through him that loved us.
For I am persuaded that neither death not life,
    Nor angels, nor principalities, nor powers,
Nor things present, nor things to come,
    Nor height, nor depth, nor any other creature,
Shall be able to separate us from the love of God,
    Which is in Christ Jesus our Lord.

Appendix E

LOVE

The Greatest of These

1 Corinthians 13

Though I speak with the tongues of men and of angels
    And have not LOVE,
I am become as sounding brass, or a tinkling cymbal.

And though I have the gift of prophecy,
    And understand all mysteries and all knowledge;

And though I have all FAITH
    So that I could remove mountains
And have not LOVE,
    I am nothing.

And though I bestow all my goods to feed the poor,
    And though I give my body to be burned,
And have not LOVE,
    It profiteth me nothing.

LOVE suffereth long,
    And is kind,
      Is not puffed up,
        Doth not behave itself unseemly,
        Seeketh not her own,
          Is not easily provoked,
           Thinketh no evil,
             Rejoiceth not in iniquity, but
             Rejoiceth in the truth;

> Beareth all things,
> Hopeth all things,
> Endureth all things.

LOVE NEVER FAILETH:

But whether there be prophecies, they shall fail;
Whether there be tongues, they shall cease;
Whether there be knowledge, it shall vanish away.

For we know in part and we prophesy in part.
But when that which is perfect is come,
Then that which is in part shall be done away.

When I was a child,
I spake as a child,
I understood as a child,
I thought as a child:

But when I became a man, I put away childish things.

For now we see through a glass darkly;
But then face to face:

Now I know in part;
But then shall I know even as I am known.

And now abideth FAITH, HOPE, LOVE,
These three;
But the greatest of these is LOVE.

Stepping Into the Light

It is time, long past time, for a whole new out-look. *Stepping into the Light* is an exciting and powerful adjustment, both spiritually and mentally, that every Christian should make!

"Dr. Wood uses all of his talents to proclaim the message of Christ the Savior. From the church pulpit or from the platform of a university the message is the same."

—Dr. Lee Roberson
Founder and Chancellor
Tennessee Temple University

"David Wood's message is personal and it is active. It has behind it the authority of history. Each time believers have stepped into the light of Christ, the work of Jesus is advanced. Try stepping into the light yourself and watch how quickly the darkness dissipates."

—Cal Thomas
Syndicated Columnist, Washington, D.C.

About the author

Dr. David Wood accepted Christ at the age of nineteen through the ministry of Dr. Jerry Falwell, pastor of the Thomas Road Baptist Church in Lynchburg, Virginia. That same year he felt the call to the ministry and left for Bible college in Three Hills, Alberta, Canada.

In 1965, he was graduated from Columbia Bible College in Columbia, South Carolina. Over the next 19 years, he founded and pastored two successful, growing, soul winning churches.

In 1984, Dr. Wood surrendered to God's call to Evangelism. He and his family are now situated on a ministry complex in Trenton, Georgia.

21st Century PRESS

P.O. Box 8087
Springfield MO 65801
1-800-658-0284